D1097159

RADICAL LIGHT

RADICAL LIGHT

Alchemy for a New World—
The Real Magic Studies

BOOK TWO

MECHANICS' INSTITUTE LIBRARY
57 Post Street
San Francisco, CA 94104
(415) 393-0101

Sylvia Bennett

Copyright © 2010 by Sylvia Bennett.

Library of Congress Control Number:		2010902404
ISBN:	Hardcover	978-1-4500-4934-4
	Softcover	978-1-4500-4933-7
	E-book	978-1-4500-4935-1

All rights reserved. No part of this book may be reproduced or transmitted in any form or by any means, electronic or mechanical, including photocopying, recording, or by any information storage and retrieval system, without permission in writing from the copyright owner.

This book was printed in the United States of America.

To order additional copies of this book, contact:
Xlibris Corporation
1-888-795-4274
www.Xlibris.com
Orders@Xlibris.com
72322

.45
72

NOV 0 4 2010

CONTENTS

MAYO CLINIC

FOREWORD

THERE ARE NO SECRETS

Ask and it shall be given. Seek and ye shall find. Knock and the door will open.
This is the Mystery School—
This is Real Magic.
No one has the center on The Way, The Truth, and The Light.
There is no secret code.
There are no secrets

I have always been fascinated by the Laws of Magic and in the year long process of the Real Magic Course, I include a class on these Laws. In this class we pay homage to and acknowledge the wisdom-keepers, the esoteric teachers who have gone before us, leaving footprints. Often in the course of my life, even as a young child, I have imagined the eons of intelligent observation, wisdom, love, and commitment to service that were required by our ancestors who had been called to the task of spiritual teacher. They spent their lives observing the working of energy and they brought their observations into forms that could be utilized by all human beings for the healing and care-taking of life on earth—forms that would allow all of us to be conscious transmuters of darkness and transmitters of Light. They have given us the tools; the information, technology, and teachings we need to work with a universe of energy and they called these tools the Laws of Magic. They created systems that allow human beings access to universal, living truths—and created laws which give coherence to the workings of Creation.

One thing that has always bothered me in my research into historical esoteric systems, and particularly the Hermetic Teachings, is the emphasis on secrecy in many of the writings on alchemy and occultism. I came to peace with this by realizing that historically the teachings were characterized by secrecy not so much because teachers considered themselves an elite company, but because the esoteric path illuminated from within the spiritual Light within each student—the Light of self-knowledge—and this is a *gnosis through direct experience* that cannot be easily interpreted and explained. The fact that it couldn't be easily talked about and shared led to superstitious fear concerning and directed toward those esoteric students who were silent in the face of the Mystery of God.

This silence created a mythology of false power around the teachings and also an atmosphere of secrecy around the teachings, an atmosphere created for the most part by those who did not seek spiritual understanding or enlightenment for themselves and whose lives and belief systems did not allow them to easily comprehend the ways of higher knowledge. Therefore, because of the atmosphere of mistrust and paranoia generated by such people, information about the Mysteries began to be deliberately withheld by the practitioners. In this way, in an attempt to guard the teachings from an ignorance that might seek to destroy them, teachers fed into this paranoia and helped to perpetuate the fear and superstition around it.

People who could not comprehend the depth of the commitment, the dedication—the deep, constant, and rigorous work required on a path of self-knowledge—came to believe that something powerful was deliberately being kept from them and this created a belief in esoteric teachings as secretive and dangerous. It is the same distrust that allowed people committed to the Creative Arts—artists, poets, and such—to be looked at as strange and even not normal, as *dangerous others*.

And historically, as organized exoteric religions formalized their dogma and consolidated their power, they utilized the concept of secrecy—secrets understood only by an elite priesthood—to intimidate and control people. They declared that only sanctified priests had the power to interpret God, and that open inquiry was threatening to the foundation of the church.

These are the energies that led to the creation of secrecy. One type of energy was the natural paranoia of the human ego when it believes that something special is being withheld from it or that special powers were being used by dangerous people against it—the belief that dangerous others were privy to secret and powerful information.

The other type of energy was the bid for power and the attack on esoteric studies created by the churches. These experiences led to an actual definition of esoteric teachings as threatening and this paranoia and the actual attacks on practitioners led to *actual and necessary* secrecy on the part of the esoteric practitioners.

In setting out to learn the Western Esoteric Tradition and create the Real Magic Course, I wanted to redeem the beautiful, misunderstood word, *magic* and to do away with the concept of secrets. I wanted to create an atmosphere of openness that would hopefully transmute the aura of secrecy around esoteric teachings and practices. Because magic and alchemy have been designated as "occult" it was difficult to find intelligent information about them. In studying the Hermetic Teachings, I had to read between a lot of occult lines to find the simplicity and depth within the actual teachings. Some beautifully intelligent tools and wonderful spiritual insights have been hidden within these esoteric and occult traditions. I understood the historical need for secrecy—(imagine being persecuted by a system like the Inquisition). But I was disappointed to find so many intelligent people today who are amazingly ignorant of the history of The Western Way—Western Mystery Traditions and the Hermetic Teachings, and even more disappointing, people who had no interest in learning. It seemed that ignorance, superstition, and the prejudice against occult studies are very entrenched in human beings and I had to fight my way through a lot of prejudice in my search for truth. I also found that as I learned to teach and worked at teaching, I had to consciously let go of any temptation in myself to use the concepts of secrecy and elitism as marketing tools to attract students.

As I researched and observed the eons of secret societies that have plagued the Western Esoteric Tradition, I began to feel deeply that the time for secrecy of any kind must come to an end. In the world, in politics and government, in the schoolyard, in the home, in the market place, in the media, where fear, ignorance, and greed are dominating energies, any attempt to diminish our human capacity to learn and choose—anything that keeps people in ignorance and paranoia—is destructive. This destructiveness is being brought to light in every aspect of today's culture. And in light of this, I find it distressing that even in today's spiritual culture, the concept of secrecy is still being used to market systems like the Hermetic Teachings and the Kabbalah and the Ancient Mysteries.

Most of the marketing in today's spiritual pop culture has to do with the ways that one can utilize spiritual practices to create prosperity. The focus of this marketing is often on material goods rather than spiritual growth and this focus appeals to human narcissism. As the state of the human species goes, this can open doors and be a step toward freedom but in the actual spiritual culture, some of the forms created by this focus on material prosperity have created fraudulent spiritual expectations and images of spiritual prosperity that look like slick magazine covers. We really don't have to gild the lily—the lily in its natural state is the Beauty of God. And we don't have to advertise—like any art form, the magic of Creation is its own attractive force.

The marketing of a new spirituality is perhaps necessary (although I would question that) but it has given rise to the belief that if you sign up for the right membership in a hip spiritual ideology, your manifest, financial prosperity will increase in manifold and miraculous ways—you will be rich and famous. This leads to high expectations, disappointment, and depression on the part of practitioners and to some extent depresses the purpose of the teachings.

I am not alone in this, many teachers are distressed by the ways that the Western Esoteric Tradition is being marketed today and by the celebrity status given to teachers and healers. But I am also aware that distracted and disenfranchised people—people who don't trust themselves—need people who stand out, need celebrities, need heroes, and therefore, need spiritual teachers to be celebrities and heroes. And if we must have heroes then let them be spiritual heroes. Spiritual heroes are as old as human need. I don't think anyone sets out to be a spiritual teacher or healer—this has always been an organic movement of the Spirit—a calling. It is unfortunate that in this market place world, financial gain has become associated with spiritual teaching and healing, this has led to a *glamour* around spiritual leaders; and to a belief that manifest prosperity has to be part of the teacher or healers' package. This is all part of a world that is in an accelerated movement toward truth and has not learned to balance itself between heaven and hell.

Marketing particular aspects of metaphysical secrets is as old as human fear—as old as human ego. Marketing that appeals to human self-importance and offers power to disenfranchised people has been characteristic of many popular esoteric and spiritual movements in the past. This created a lot of paranoia and competition within the latter half of the 19th century in the spiritual atmosphere of the time. This was a carry-over from the Middle Ages that has carried over into today's esoteric aura. We are still, today, being influenced by the attacks on esoteric studies at the turn of the century.

The truth is that there is no such thing as a spiritual secret. So I find it distressing that because there is so much hype used in marketing esoteric packages, the word secret, instead of dying away as it would in a healthy society, is having a resurgence. It is good that in the mainstream spiritual culture, people are beginning to realize just what the ancient esoteric teachings on alchemy such as The Hermetica or The Kabbalah, really have to offer. The old teachings are describing and offering a technology for the actual and authentic transmutation of energy—wherein form itself could be created and form could equally be dissolved. And these ancient teachings are focused on walking a Path to God. This is a technology of Love and not on the same page as secret societies.

We need the many faces of Love. It is no accident that the Dalai Lama's face is everywhere. At this point in time the human ego has become so fear-driven that if it is *not* showered with truth, beauty, intelligence and love, it could destroy the forms of life most cherished by true lovers on this beautiful planet. This is a good advertisement for choosing Compassion and above all, a Path of Freedom for all Beings.

I was attracted to the Western Esoteric Studies, particularly the Hermetic Teachings, because I have a *passion* for Freedom. I found in these studies a Path toward *Freedom* that resonated with every revolutionary, heart-felt cry of every true rebel who has ever been fierce on behalf of Freedom—like Jesus—and Hermes. A passion for Freedom is a great motivator toward truth.

Long before a secular European intellectualism discovered Hermes, before the first chemist took Hermes into the laboratory and made the teachings earthbound, before the Teachings became A Secret, they were pure, and they were The Word of God. Pure gold. I fell in love with the intensity of Hermes, with the depth of these Teachings, how deep they can go, how constant they remain, how much they make possible for the wounded soul—from God's mouth to my heart, these Teachings are the most beautiful gift God has ever given to the wanderers in the wasteland of humanity.

There are no secrets. The Hermetic Teachings were freely given and we have been free, generation after generation, to re-create these teachings through many teachers and through whatever forms speak most heartfully to us. I have tried to recreate the pure teachings, a technology of Love that was created for the purpose of working with consciousness itself and which can change consciousness itself if used purely.

SECRECY

According to Roget's the following words are all associated with the word "secret": *covert; clandestine; stealthy; furtive; surreptitious; underhanded; etc.*

None of these words apply to the Creative Process. This process is the same whether you are manifesting war and poverty or peace and prosperity. Control or freedom, it is all the same process and it cannot be controlled because this creative process is out of human hands. *It cannot be distorted by human ego.* Only *intention* can be distorted by human beings.

It is true that various societies and religions of the human world have tried to control access to God by creating dogmas that deny the simplicity of God. *(I use the word God to mean the Universal, Conscious, Vastly Intelligent, and All-Pervading, Divine Creative Energy that brings all of life into being and is characterized by a vast, universal, all pervading, no-strings-attached Conscious Love).* The truth is that Human beings *are* the Creative Process—the Word made flesh. Human beings *are* the Great Work. Human beings *are* Alchemists. *All human beings have access to eternity.*

The Eternal Universal Teachings have been with us always. The Eternal Teachings are not a mass movement—the teachings are made comprehensive by individual human beings choosing to consciously transmute their own personal relationship with Creation and create within themselves a state of Freedom.

The true state of human consciousness can be summed up in the words of Hermes Trismegistus, who foretold the state of the suffering ego and what the human ego would create in regard to the Great Work. These words from Hermes are from the translation of *The Hermetica* by Timothy Freke and Peter Gandy.

"*Wise words, although written by my decaying hand, remain imperishable through time; imbued with the medicine of immortality by the All-Master,*

Be unseen and undiscovered by all those who will come and go, wandering the wastelands of life. Be hidden, until an older heaven births human beings who are worthy of your wisdom."

Unseen, undiscovered—these words refer to a treasure that must be uncovered from within, bit by bit, as the human being, like the hero in an ancient fairy tale, walks the path through her or his own tangled egoland, and as they walk, they transmute the dark, ego-affirming beliefs and subsequent emotions that live in this human wasteland. One offers one's self to Creation and surrenders one's ego with pure intention and trust to the Radiant Awareness, Pure Love, Awesome Intelligence and Imperishable Truth that has, for countless eons, Guided and Guarded human beings. This is the Manifest Truth that moved Hermes to say, *Oh God, you sing so beautifully through me.*

Buddha declared that Benign Celestials watch over those who wander the wastelands of life. Gratitude. Gratitude to the Masters. Keepers of the Dream. Teachers. God's poets and God's artists. They have kept nothing secret, have withheld nothing, waiting patiently for us to uncover our own sacred Self—the creativity of the human heart and the freedom of the human mind and Spirit. This Universal Intention is a Radiant Fellowship. There are no secrets.

INTRODUCTION
BEYOND WORDS

This book has been inspired by the alchemy that comes into play between student and teacher when the student asks a question and the teacher becomes a conduit. These examples are from actual Seminars that I have taught and taped for years. Seminars are different from the formal Real Magic Course classes in that they are open-ended and provide an opportunity for students to ask questions and discuss aspects of the Course that aren't addressed in the formal classes.

This excerpt, "Beyond Words", is from a Seminar that was taped shortly after the first Real Magic book—Magic; The Simple Truth, was released in 2004. I had at the time been receiving many questions pertaining to the release of the book and in this Seminar I addressed these questions. As I was reading through the transcript, I realized that it would make a good introduction to this book.

Welcome.

The Real Magic book *(Magic; The Simple Truth)* is now available. Several of you have asked me to suggest ways to describe and discuss the book with your friends and family. I understand that it is difficult for you to talk about the Real Magic Course—there is no theory or philosophy that you can use to explain it to people. Your experiences in the Course are so deep, so intimate, so beyond words, that it is difficult to talk about them at a mental or interpretive level. You cannot theorize about the Course because it is so intimately about you and your experience of transformation.

At the same time, you don't want to present it in a way that will be misinterpreted; that will give people the impression that studying this work has made you special.

What is the Real Magic Course? It is a set of ancient principles and practices which—as you utilize these principles and practices—create a spiritual path. This path is designed by your own unique individuality, therefore it is a path that you create for yourself by doing the practices and studying the principles. As you do the practices, a Path unfolds that did not exist until you began practicing it.

So the Real Magic Course is a path of transformation that is created by your own experience as you go step by step through the Course practicing the principles. This is very difficult to discuss theoretically—it is a Pathless Path—there are no signposts—you create the signposts as you go.

This makes it difficult to theorize about. I had the same problem with writing a book about the Course. When I was looking for a starting point, I did not know how to begin a book that is beyond words and which begins right in the center of where you are at.

In attempting to create a book about the Course I found myself going back to my initial inspirations; reconnecting with the Hermetic Teachings and my feelings and thoughts about alchemy. I reconnected with why I was so drawn to these disciplines in the first place.

Why? I wanted to learn to transmute energy! I have *always* known that *we*, human beings, could *directly*, with our minds, our thoughts, and our desire for truth, transmute energy and change the world. With my first revelation I perceived at once how revolutionary this teaching is. And I learned as I studied that the ideas that create the most interference with simply transmuting energy is our human obsession with "*how; prove it, and interpret it (what does it mean?)*" How can energy be transmuted? I began to feel that only if we become *energetically conscious* in our attempts to change the world for the better—if we develop a conscious awareness of the *energetics* involved, only then could the changes be authentically true and powerful and nurturing for *everyone*.

So I pursued the study of alchemy as a technology that deals with subtle energies, which, once learned, would allow people to directly and consciously transmute the energy of their own consciousness and in so doing, transmute the consciousness within the planet itself. And such transmutation happens in an organic way. The Hermetic Teachings provide a path—a path that never loses touch with nature, never loses touch with one's own creativity as it moves in a natural, organic way following cosmic laws.

In the beginning, as I pursued alchemical and esoteric studies I was very frustrated with what was at the time available. As I studied, I had revelations about the Hermetic Teachings and realized that these teachings—and Hermes in all his guises down through the ages—were offering us a Technology of Love. And in a Technology of Love you can change anything under the sun—Authentic Change—because you change things through grace and organic movement and not through unnatural manipulation or violent disruption. Once that Technology of Love becomes a part of you, you connect with your truest self and walk in an existence that is true to you because you are consciously creating it and you *know* that you are consciously creating it.

So what can you say about these books or about the Course—say that the Path of Real Magic offers a Technology of Love—an always creative and interesting Path of Light through the shadowy jungle of collective ego forms—thought-forms that haunt us personally and haunt the planet.

*   *   *

We are studying The Great Work—and the goal of the Great Work is, of course, the transmutation of conflict into harmonious wholeness. This requires the transmutation of the human ego. I based the Course on a Hermetic Principle—*that opposite, even contradictory, states of being can unite harmoniously through the transmuting action of a new Word*. Trash into Treasure. This new Word is a new Intention that *structures* available energy and calls forth an entirely new potential from the old form.

So the Course is this: using the Principle of Attention to create energy, we focus on the Principle of Polarity and Intention to give the energy a structure. In structuring the energy we are able to direct it toward a desired result. We use mantras and power points to keep the structure moving toward that desired result.

I also subscribe to the Hermetic belief that human beings have a Divine Origin, an Original Blessing, and because humans originated from the Word of God, humans are creative beings imbued with a God-spark, a Superconscious potential for constant, radiant awareness. The Superconscious mind is the faculty through which humans are able to comprehend and utilize God's Word—and thereby consciously participate in the evolution of life—the transmutation of matter into Spirit. Therefore the second half of the Real Magic Course covers Energy Studies and the Superconscious. But that is another book.

There are many teachers and teachings now based on the idea that form follows thought and that whatever thoughts you dwell on will manifest in your life. This is why I focus on qualities and states of being rather than material goods. There are enough teachers focused on material wealth. And academic alchemy is focused on laboratory work with chemical elements and physical results. This is the old world. Let us focus The Great Work on manifesting qualities like trust, wisdom, compassion, and being true to ones' Self. A New World. You can argue that qualities are not form—well, qualities are not material form but a quality is *tangible* and when you have chosen to receive a quality—such as compassion—and it manifests within you, you *feel* it, you *know* it is there—it is unmistakable—it is you—and you are *for real* Real Magic.

CHAPTER ONE

THE LAWS OF MAGIC

I always meant to tape a class on the ancient Laws of Magic but never got around to it so, although I taught the class, I have no transcript of interaction with students. So I am presenting as this first Chapter the essay I wrote as a handout for the class on the Laws of Magic.

THE LAWS OF MAGIC

"Law;—8. a) a sequence of events in nature or in human activities that has been observed to occur with unvarying uniformity under the same conditions b) the formulation in words of such a sequence;

11. a divine commandment.

The Great Universal Teachings have been with us from the dawning of human consciousness. These teachings are based on universal laws that describe the basic workings of energy that govern all life in Creation—they describe the human relationship with God and the simplicity of the Path to God. In my teaching I have tried to describe the Creative Process in ways that will allow human beings to easily and simply understand and utilize these teachings.

Eons ago the masters who laid out the Universal teachings documented all the variables that influence the universal workings of energy and made them into working principles which have been passed down through the centuries. These Principles appear in every culture from the Egyptian, the Upanishads, through the Kabbala, the Tree of Life and the Tarot. These Laws of Magic are all descriptions of *energy doing things.*

The only conscious *law* I refer to in the Real Magic Course is the Law of Definition. *The Law of Definition: whatever you define and dwell on most consistently in your conscious and unconscious thoughts and feelings will be attracted to you, and it will manifest in your life because by the Law of Definition, it is yours—meaning it vibrates to your frequency, and will appear in your life in some form or another because you have defined it—your definition of it has given it form and your attention on it has given it shape and color.*

Here are just a few of these Laws of Magic. If you were studying Shamanism from any culture, or Western Ritual Magic, or "Magick" of any kind you would be learning and practicing each of these Laws along with numerous other rules and regulations that cover all possible situations where focused attention releases energy and creates a shift that leads to change. Ritual magic and laboratory alchemy is particularly loaded with pedantic *"right way to do it"* rules.

Imagine having to learn each of the following Laws before you could begin to practice Real Magic. These are the Laws of Energy and can all come under the heading of *Energy Doing Things.* Look at these Laws and see if you can connect them to the teachings in The Real Magic Course.

The Law of Definition
The Law of Words of Power
The Law of Knowledge
The Law of Cause and Effect
The Law of Polarity (The Law of Magnetism)
The Law of Attraction
The Law of Vibration
The Law of Invocation (from within)
The Law of Evocation (from without)
The Law of Contagion
The Law of Similarity
The Law of Identification
The Law of Personification
The Law of Synthesis
The Law of Reversal
The Law of Balance

The basis for all the Laws of Magic is that they all work and they are all true. But how ponderous, outdated and unnecessary they are once you understand the Law of Definition. *"As you call it, so it shall be."* If you define it, it is yours, if you keep paying attention to it (focusing energy on it), it will come into your life in some form or another. The form in which it comes into your life is often determined by something I call the *Law of the Spanner in the Works,* or, Creation always has the last word.

How about; *a thing becomes what it is repeatedly called.* This could become a maxim for the raising of children. Call them good, call them joy, call them blessing, call them luminous intelligence, call them courage, call them sweet. Over and over again, call them sweet.

How about; *whether it is a demon or an angel, it is your own self-fulfilling prophecy coming into being through the laws of energy.* The Universe is an ocean of blessing or a sea of trial and tribulation depending on where you are standing, how you perceive it to be—how you *define* it. To define is to create. To create is to embody. You attract what you *embody.* You call it and you become it, you become it and it is yours. This buck cannot be passed. It stops here with something called *personal accountability.*

The trick is to accept that you are responsible for the choices you make *and* at the same time accept that *there is no blame.* You are not going to be punished if you make a wrong choice because there is no such thing as a wrong choice. You are simply going to continue on in a school of your own making—I prefer to call it a *path*—until you get it all balanced under "The Law of Being True to Yourself." Or enlightenment, or aged to perfection—whichever you prefer to call it, the truth about yourself and the truth about Creation are one and the same and this truth is your most treasured possession.

You are an alchemist. A Creative Matrix. You are the Crucible, the Sacred Vessel, the Philosophers Stone, and the Holy Grail. Everything you want to transmute is within your vessel. Everything you want to create is within you.

You are an elegant alchemy. You are the vessel within which the transmutation of energy takes place. What gets transmuted in this vessel of yourself? The emotional content you carry and the belief that this emotional content is *truth* gets transmuted. The belief that you are separate from God gets transmuted. The belief that you are a victim gets transmuted. The belief that you are not loved gets transmuted. Your relationship with the world gets transmuted. Your relationship with your Self gets transmuted. Your trash gets transmuted. Transmuted to what? Treasure.

This is the purpose of every human being on earth. To turn trash into Treasure on the most beautiful home planet we will ever experience. The earth is beautiful. The Beauty of Earth is the Beauty of God made manifest—in the flesh—the culmination of God's Dream. We are the Beautiful Dreamers—if we can make it so and we make it so by dreaming it into being. This is a simple truth. There are no secrets in an open heart. We Are Here To Be the Open Heart of Creation.

CHAPTER TWO

ATTENTION; THE POWER OF FOCUS; AN IMPORTANT FOCUS; THE MOST POWERFUL SKILL; FEELINGS; BELIEFS AND EGO

The next few chapters are from transcripts of actual Seminars. The Seminars I teach are different from the Real Magic Course classes in that they are less formal, more open ended, and there is room for more commentary from the students.

Question from student: *"Would you talk about attention—why is attention so important? I know 'It's the most powerful thing we have' but why is that so? What makes it powerful?"*

The process of creation requires only one thing—it requires energy—*a lot* of energy—tremendous, unimaginable, amounts of energy. And where does the energy that we use creatively come from? It comes from our *focused attention*. Anyplace, any point in the Universe where your attention is focused will be a gathering place for *tremendous* energies. In order to turn this tremendous build up of energy into tangible form, this energy must be *focused on an intention*. Energy is created *wherever* our attention remains focused in a deliberate or conscious way. Form is created wherever our attention remains focused on an *intention*.

Energy is *also* created when our attention is focused in an *unconscious* way such as the energies that emanate from our deep beliefs—or from obsession—which can either be negative and dark or wonderfully creative as any artist driven to create a particular work of art can tell you.

So through our human ability to focus our attention a tremendous build-up of energy can occur. Then as you focus this energy on an Intention, this Intention; this *Word*; becomes a container that holds this focused energy and as the energy builds, a form that represents this Intention can come into being. The Hawaiian Kahuna say that if you *call—(focus on and hold)*—a word, Creation responds with an equivalent word.

So—if you keep your attention directed so that it stays focused—for example, if your point A is anger and you focus on Serenity and keep your attention focused on Serenity—you can create a tremendous amount of the energy of Serenity. And the energy of Serenity that you create through your attention builds and builds, pouring into the *structure—the Word*—you have created to hold it—and Serenity manifests as a true and lasting part of you and your existence.

What do I mean by structure? How do you create a structure that guides, holds and directs the energy? This is what the Principle of Polarity is for. Using the Principle of Polarity you state what you want to let go of (Point A). Then you state a new intention at the *opposite* point (B). This gives you a structure. Then you focus attention on the new *Intention (Point B)*. What is an Intention?

A Word. *"In the beginning was the Word."* A Word which, emanating from you, becomes a Word of Power—a mantra—which holds and structures and gives form to all the available focused creative energy you can summon.

So—why is attention the most powerful thing you have? If you learn to use your attention consciously, you can gather and hold vast energies and direct those energies into manifest form. It is the Law. Your Word of Power has your signature on it. It knows its creator. Serenity—or whatever you choose to create—will always be yours because it is your conscious creation.

And—why is *intention* such a powerful force? You can create a lot of energy with your attention but if that energy you've gathered has no place to go it just dissipates and all you can do is stay attached to process and keep telling yourself the same old story. The gathering of energy needs the Principle of Polarity and the Power of the Word to give it form. Focusing on an *intention* tells this focused energy what to do—it gives it a basic structure like a skeleton gives a basic structure to a human body, and a wooden frame gives a structure to a house you are building. Point B is the focal point for *gathering and containing* the energy that will build the form that you are calling into being. Focus your attention on a clear intention and keep it focused—all the practices and principles in the Course build on this simple truth. The simple truth of magic. This is why I say there are no secrets.

Student: *"Then why isn't everyone studying this? Mainstream spiritual teachings seem to be focused more on spiritual psychology and on studying the psyche from a scientific point of view. What is different in you—that you don't focus on outcomes?—or on manipulating material wealth?"*

The primary difference is that I have never focused on *marketing* because marketing has to be focused through an appeal that reaches the human ego. I have never held out a carrot to the human ego. I have even turned people away from my classes. I focus on attracting a few people who are ready for the rigorous and subtle work of the Real Magic Course—or which any esoteric path like the Course—requires.

And I am focused on my love for a lineage. There is a great lineage of teachers and adepts that goes back long before Jesus or Solomon or Abraham, back to universal teachings in the form of a teacher or teachers who are so far removed in time that they remain unknown, they remain as Gods. We know them in the form of Thoth and Hermes—Egyptian Masters who created teachings inspired directly by God. We call these teachings The Hermetic Teachings. In legend, Hermes Trismegistus was reported to be congruent with Thoth and legend says that Thoth was the first incarnation of the First Teachings which we have come to know as the Hermetic Teachings. This teacher was given the name Hermes Trismegistus by the Greeks who associated him with their God Hermes—the Greek equivalent to the Egyptian Thoth. Legend also has it that Hermes was the teacher of Abraham who in turn formulated and taught his people The Tree of Life and the beginnings of the collective teachings that became the Kabbalah. And legend also has it that Hermes—and this is what Trismegistus refers to—reincarnates in each new era, inspiring teachers who create new and pertinent forms of The Hermetic Teachings. The Real Magic Course is a new and pertinent to the times re-creation.

One form of that lineage—*the form I most resonate with and love*—is a belief that a teacher should remain anonymous—in terms of advertising—and quietly teach small groups of people who are committed to going as far as is possible to go into one deep well of teachings. It is a characteristic of this lineage that adepts stay with it for lifetimes, and through this handful of teachings they go as deep as they need to go and learn All-Knowledge—everything there is to learn because they walk a Path that leads to Self as Thou; as God.

The Hermetic Teachings are so ancient and so simple and direct that no one believes them so there have to be Courses and classes created and many teachers saying in various ways that manifesting or the transmutation of energy requires your focused attention and a clear intention. And in today's world of distraction, this requires a lot of loud and colorful mass marketing and this marketing must appeal to the ego, must make claims that will offer the ego a place in a unique and elite company. Such as—*it's a Specialized Secret and if you know the Key you will be very special! And we are the ones who know the Key so sign up with us!*

I find myself unable to create this kind of sales pitch. Taking the Simplicity and Beauty of Creation and the Creative Process and selling it as a specialized skill and a secret that gives power to the holder is a hype, a marketing manipulation. It makes me feel the way Jesus must have felt when he picked up a whip and drove the profiteers out of the temple courtyard. There are no secrets—this beauty of Creation is our human birthright. Our job is to do the rigorous work required to embody the Great Work.

How do you consciously create an existence that your heart longs for? You gather the most powerful thing you have and make it work for you by utilizing the most powerful force in the universe. That's the basic Real Magic Course right there.

Student: *"Then wouldn't Focus be the most powerful thing we have and the most powerful study?"*

Well, to be accurate you could say that *conscious focus* is the most powerful *skill* we can learn. Focus is a verb that refers to an ability—a skill—and a skill is something that can be *learned*. Attention is something we *have*—something inherent in our consciousness. Even a mentally challenged person has power in their attention. But they often have a *disruption* in their focusing skills. A short attention span can be changed into a long and powerful attention span—but we all—all humans—have an attention span. Focus is something we can all learn to do—but we are not all naturally talented in focusing skills, we have to *practice and perfect it for within our focused attention is self-knowledge*. And *"Know Thyself"* is the most important form of knowledge there is.

And the single most important quality of that word focus is that it is *not* emotional, it does not depend on emotion for its power in the way that our beliefs and obsessions do. In a conscious focus, there is no processing, there is only the action—the stillness of truth—in the moment. So if you are focused on processing emotions and interpreting feelings, you are not consciously focused on transmutation—you are living in your fear or hurt or anger or greed, and you are focused on fear of lack and fear of damage—you are living in and processing the past.

Don't do this. The past has already happened, it needs no more energy from you—it needs the energy of revelation—which, in a moment; in the twinkling of an eye, comes to you from a conscious focus on spiritual practices and a constant commitment to doing those practices the way they are presented to you.

A matured ability to focus your attention creates a constant state of being. State of Being does not mean *thinking about* being, it means *Being*. Focus your Attention does not mean think about your attention, it means *be* your attention.

Student: *"Then what would you say is the most important thing to focus attention on in the Course? I mean as we work, follow through, the Course?"*

Do the practices! Do the practices continually and constantly. *Do all the practices equally.* There is no one practice that is more powerful than any other. All the practices are powerful, but if you take them out of the context of the Teachings, *the energy will dissipate.* So one of the practices is to study the Teachings. So—again—*do all the practices equally*—this can't be stressed enough. Some people only do the practices when they feel bad—because that is the only time they remember that they want things to change and of course this will eventually reinforce—feed—the very thing they would like to transmute. This goes against the very concept of transmutation—you don't just work on change when you feel bad, *you work all the time.* And you let go of any focus on process or analysis. The Work has nothing to do with processing self-importance. Processing is not The Work but it is easy for a student to fall back on process because this is familiar and makes them feel better, makes them feel that something is happening.

Power points are the opposite of processing. Power points, actually all the practices, are not supposed to make you feel better, *they are supposed to raise enough energy toward your new intentions that the new gathered and contained energy causes the energy of your old intentions to dissipate.* The practices are given to you for the one and clear purpose of transmuting your old self. This is why it is counter productive to focus on your feelings.

This is the way to create powerful change—change that is powerful enough to restructure your brain and to restructure your ego. These methods are the opposite of psychological processing. The practices are designed to bypass the ego and transmute it at the same time you are bypassing it. The practices are simple, the principles are easy to grasp—hold your attention on a Word and this creates energy and structure; stay focused on this Word by using a mantra and that structure will fill with the energy of Creation, and you will manifest something. It is literal and simple. Yes . . . ?

Student: *"So 'simple but not easy' is literally true. Could you elaborate on why it doesn't happen this literally and easily?"*

Why doesn't this happen easily? Because of human self-importance. A part of your own consciousness won't allow it to happen easily. Your ego won't let it, your ego is programmed to control everything in your existence and the very nature of our work requires you to deliberately let go of control—let go of *wanting to control anything.* This brings up your fear and when your fear comes up, you believe it is real, therefore, you have resistance. Resistance happens in the place where the ego is in charge. This is the hardest part of the Work, releasing the ego so that it can be transmuted.

Your ego uses your belief in fear—look at yourself, you believe that your fear is real—don't you? And it certainly feels real. Any deep emotional attachment is going to *feel real.* Your emotional attachment to that belief and your attachment to safety control your existence. Why? In your world of ego-thought, the polarity of fear is *safety.* On the other hand, in the world of truth, the polarity of fear is *fearless.*

There are many different ways we define safety and fearless and we have to work through the *felt energy* of those old definitions. To transmute fear to fearless and live in truth is the goal of your Authentic Self. But your egoic consciousness has a dictionary that does not include fearless—you could even say it classifies fearless as a "dangerous other." So—your ego is doing its job, doing what it evolved to do. Now our job is to restructure the ego and take it into the next step of evolution. Evolution being, in this definition, a word that describes the process of the ego moving towards truth. So evolution is no big deal, it is only a process—it has little to do with Truth—with true Creation. We have discussed this many times. I mean how do you define evolution? Some people define the discovery of nuclear power and technology as successful evolution. I define evolution as the successful transmutation of the ego from a fearful, self-important being into a being of serenity, compassion, and wisdom. And this will happen because evolution is a movement of Divine Design that has its own agenda and moves in divine order and in perfect timing. It doesn't really need any help from us. WE need help from us, evolution doesn't. I just want to accelerate Freedom.

Student: *"Could you discuss ego one more time. What do you mean by ego—or how do you in particular define ego?"*

Ego is a word that refers to an aspect of human consciousness that is for the most part unconscious. I use it to define the unconscious parts of yourself and how this unconsciousness functions within your larger consciousness. Ego is a consciousness. It is a consciousness that lives within and is a part of our total human consciousness—it is a part of, not apart from. It is a small piece of your reality yet the nature of this egoic reality includes a belief that this small piece of your reality is the whole thing, the real deal. It is a consciousness that is focused on separateness. It functions according to a belief that safety lies in staying separate from danger and anything known and unknown in Creation can be defined by the ego as dangerous.

The ego is like an organ—like the heart or liver—an organ that has a strong *intention*—an intention that resides deep within our consciousness. This intention is a program that instructs our personal, individual, ego; tells it to protect our identity, our integrity—it is a program that keeps us intact and it keeps us knowing how to respond to a world of dangerous others. This program tells our ego to protect our physical body and to protect our belief systems—the clusters of belief that are stored in our energy field. In this way, by protecting our beliefs, our ego protects our identity.

Why do we need it? Why did it evolve? To maintain a coherent human *identity*. What is the point of being here if we cannot remain intact long enough to learn Wisdom? Keeping your identity intact as it exists right now requires that your belief systems—everything you believe to be true about reality—must be protected. And to do this, it—the ego—draws on past experiences—ego is never in the moment, it is always drawing on and living in the past. If it wasn't orientated toward the past it would not know what to protect

This egoic consciousness corresponds to the subconscious and unconscious parts of your energy. It is unseen but it is a powerful energy structure and a powerful guiding force in human consciousness. It can hold fear in and keep trust out simply because its job is to protect your identity—and it—this program—protects your identity by keeping it stable, by *not allowing your consciousness to change.*

If you have a lot of fear agendas, your ego is going to function in a way that keeps this fear from shifting or leaving. Why? Because the ego is programmed to hold a belief that the fear is a real and important part of your identity—and ego is protecting the fear *because* the ego is protecting your identity. The ego is about *identity*. You constantly identify yourself to yourself through your ego. Even if the fear is killing you, your ego will protect the fear because the fear defines and identifies you. Isn't that a sobering thought? Do you want fear to be your reason for being? Fear can be transmuted. Believe this.

The human ego is a consciousness that was designed for the purpose of protecting the physical form, and your egoic program has to do with the ability to remember trauma and create a belief in danger based on your experiences and what you tell yourself about each experience you have. Your ego maintains a file of possible dangerous others and you are always chattering to yourself about this file and constantly sorting out and interpreting all possible potential dangerous others—as if mentally you believe that you have to keep track of damage and you have to keep track of dangerous others. Your ego is a boy-scout—always prepared.

Think of the first time, as a child, you reached to pick up a hot coal from a camp fire or touched a hot stove. Imagine the energy that surged through you. I'm sure you never touched it again and you learned to say "owie" and "hot" and you never forgot it. Imagine being two years old and falling into water that closes over your head. *And whoever pulls you out of the water is freaking out!* Very bad experience! Just once and you never do it again. And you might retain the belief that water—or fire—is a *dangerous other* for lifetimes. Why? Because your ego has the ability to file a belief and pass those beliefs on. Person by person, tribe by tribe, culture by culture it maintains these files of beliefs about what a human being is and how the human being should be in the face of the many dangerous others we are likely to encounter. These are collective energies, which create a whole body of energy that we—whole families, whole communities, whole countries—draw on for how to live and be in a potentially dangerous world. But it is not the beliefs themselves that are bad.

Beliefs are not bad. The bad thing about beliefs is that they become *emotional certainties about our identity*—your identity about being a child, or being a man or a woman, or being white, or being black, or being red, or yellow, or being fat, or being thin, or being bad, or being good, etc—all this is held in your deepest emotional being. Whatever the belief—positive or negative—your ego will hold on to that belief because your ego is programmed to hold on—hold on or die—and especially the ego holds to the belief that you must never be wrong, it is deadly, lethal, the worst thing in the world is to be wrong, *your identity must not be wrong!*

These are deep emotional certainties you are carrying. And these emotional certainties are powerful and we cling to them and fight to hold on to them and believe that if we don't protect our racial, tribal, cultural, identity, our beliefs about who we are and what is right, we will stop existing. So we are programmed to kill or die for this program. Yes . . . (nods to student with raised hand).

Student: *"I'm not sure I get this . . . does the ego think?"*

No. The ego doesn't *think* in the sense of reasoning things out. It is a part of our being that functions *energetically*, as a *vibration* programmed to recognize and protect any vibration that resonate with the program while rejecting vibrations that don't resonate with the program—these *outside other* vibrations would resonate a kind of *red alert* to the ego. Look at it as if—when the ego was evolving it functioned as a one, a two, and a three vibration and protected the human parts which existed within that one to three resonance.

As the human being evolved, the ego evolved and eventually came to reside in us as a program that protected any part of our being that was vibrating between a one to five degree vibration. Anything outside of the five—and that five is basically the astral world—is now a possible dangerous other. And since we are such intelligent, creative beings, we worked out many variables on this survival mode. For example: the ego had programmed a fear of fire and deep water, while it also had a fear of cold and a fear of thirst so it evolved a subtle understanding that water and fire were necessary to our well being but water and fire were dangerous and had to be controlled—and we worked out the many ways that nature—or any possible dangerous other—could be controlled—this is how subtle the ego is in the world of vibration. Then, in the course of things, the ego had to expand to incorporate a fear of electricity while understanding that certain frequencies of *contained* electricity are benign and essential to our well-being. So we became more and more sophisticated as we learned how to control our environment in order to survive.

Now we are asking this part of our consciousness to once again expand in a conscious way and expand step by step into the highest vibration of being the human can reach. For example, imagine that the superconscious frequency is a nine/ten vibration and therefore the ego must now expand from a five vibration into a ten and do this very quickly in the midst of a highly complex, deeply polarized world.

Therefore, what is damaging is not the fact that we have ego or have beliefs—it is our relationship to belief itself that is damaging—it is our ability to cling to beliefs that is damaging. In other words—attachment! Damage is caused by our attachments. Our attachments feed our ego and our ego feeds the information within the attachment back to us—strengthening the attachment and maintaining the loop. This relationship of attachment to beliefs has created a planet of separation, of beliefs fighting with other beliefs . . .

Student: *"Maintaining the loop . . . What does that mean? The ego feeds our attachment back to us . . . ?"*

Yes. It is simple. Have you ever noticed the competitive, "prove it!" aspects of yourself? Yes?

Student: *"You mean the freak out that happens if we are accused of being wrong or if we are afraid that we are wrong? Or our dread of losing face or losing status?"* (student laughter)

Yes! If we are attached to anything, this attachment creates huge amounts of *unconscious* attention. This attention *attracts* the proof we need if we are going to retain (and believe in) the beliefs that hold our current identity together. Carrying and holding a belief requires proof—validation that the belief is correct and unshakable and strong. This is why there is such a strong desire within the ego to enlist other people, gather others of the same vibrational frequency around us.

The ego has to be right. Yes . . . ? Attachment leads us into *attracting proof* and the proof strengthens the belief and this maintains the loop between—belief > ego > proof = stronger belief > stronger attachment = stronger ego. This is where the energy within a power point comes into the play of forces. *Using power points breaks the ego loop and prevents the ego from constantly bringing our vibration back to the frequency of our most current belief system. Power Points interfere with the frequency of the identity the ego is guarding. This is why so much fear arises when we embark on a path of transformation. We come face to face with our most entrenched belief clusters.*

And the worst energy we carry is the bottom line belief that any potential *other* might prove to be a *dangerous* other and therefore all *others* must be controlled lest they turn out to be dangerous. This fundamental belief has created a species that is programmed to believe that fear is real and that dangerous others are real and that dangerous others must be kept under control—a species that believes that its feelings of threat and danger are real. We've become a species that responds to threat with the energy of control. This is, among other destructive things, very time-consuming. It consumes us.

This way of thought created a species that is psychologically programmed to believe that its *feelings* should be trusted. This belief guides our psycho/mental thought process. Very scary. Does this encourage trust between human beings? No. A belief in dangerous others and a belief that we must trust the feelings that this belief engenders, does not inspire trust.

Student: *"But we are taught that our feelings are the realest thing we have. Isn't this true?"*

No it is not true! This focus on feelings is cultural and very twentieth century. It came into being with the onset of a psychological interpretation of life. Your choices—conscious and unconscious—are the realest things you have and the more conscious your choices are—and by conscious I mean coming from self-knowledge—the more powerful, present, and authentic you are. *Your feelings are simply an indication that your belief system is active—and this activation can be biological, cellular, mental, or emotional—it is still only an indication of energy doing things.*

When a belief has been tapped and energized, the *information stored in that belief* takes over and expresses as *feelings. And you are going to react to these feelings as if they are reality because feelings are visceral and you cannot ignore feelings.* These feelings that arise in you are both personal and collective. These feelings were created, originated from once powerful raw emotion emanating from raw experience, so the source of some of your deep and often unconscious beliefs and subsequent feelings originated as a powerful emotional impact. The reality of your beliefs make themselves felt in your feelings and those feelings and beliefs were born from emotional experience—it is powerful emotional impact that creates beliefs. Sometimes our reactions activate us to escape from real physical danger. But in the main, feelings are the way your egoic consciousness communicates its definition of reality.

If you believe that your feelings are real and that you must trust them, then you are going to be feeding and holding on to some very old, negative beliefs about yourself and about life in the world and your ego will be very strong. The stronger your ego is the more powerful will be the feelings that feed your self-importance. And the stronger your ego is, the more powerful will be the belief that your feelings are *important*.

(This makes you a normal twenty-first century human being who needs, as most people do, therapy—because life is just too frightening without someone to help you process your interpretations of life. This is all right. There is nothing wrong with therapy or with needing it. And I often say that not many people are ready for the Real Magic Course because it is focused on autonomy.) The Course requires you to accept—with no explanation or interpretation—that your feelings are not important in themselves—your feelings are only *information*.

This is why we commit to the Great Work, which is, to transmute everything within ourselves that creates fear, distrust, anger, and war—to *transmute* our *feelings*—to search within ourselves, to find and heal our self-hatred, the *dangerous other* within ourselves—the *wounded* ego—to transmute the feelings of self-importance that we carry like banners into the world. Not to analyze and interpret feelings but to transmute them. Very scary. To the ego, the thought of transmuting feelings is very scary.

The reason we must work so hard to learn discernment, to practice compassion, to create goodness in ourselves is because we are working against a planetary point A—basic, bottom line, internal, cellular, planetary, collective beliefs that create tremendous fear—fear of loss, damage, and danger, and a powerful belief that victim is real and that we must, for our own safety, hold on to and process our victim consciousness—these beliefs are lodged in the human collective.

Each human being carries a structure of beliefs that at any moment can trigger a reaction within us *the moment we feel that we are not safe.* And this is why we can't just focus our attention on a *new* intention and have it come into being. As soon as we focus on a new Word—and that new Word will contain a new frequency—our egoic consciousness begins fighting the frequency—fighting the vibration of that new Word—fighting our new choices, resisting our spiritual practices. Then our feelings go into conflict, feelings of panic and paranoia arise, and those feelings tell us to blame and destroy some dangerous other. This is what we have to contend with and why we must be strong and determined if we want to manifest real change on this planet. A Great Work indeed!

The Course practices are continually teaching us a new way of thought, new ways to process information and to believe that we have other and greater options, and that for the sake of all beings, we can focus on and bring into being those other options.

Student: *"So do we have to rid ourselves of all beliefs? Isn't that possibly dangerous? And is it possible? Is this why the Eastern religions say 'slay the ego'?"*

"Slay the ego" is an ancient teaching that arose in a particular time and place, in a particular culture that likely needed to hear it taught in that particular way. As a Western spiritual teacher I have an entirely different thought process. No, the ego is *not* a dangerous *other*—so do *not* try to kill the ego, this can feed your self-condemnation until you hate yourself for having an ego or for having a bad, lower self. "Slay the ego" is a violent judgment against yourself. "Slay the ego" can create even more separation. We can't really, in this human form, exist without an ego.

The ego is an amazing invention. It is an intelligent force but it functions unconsciously, just as our Spirit is an intelligent force that functions superconsciously. This is what I mean when I say that when you transmute your ego, you are taking what is unconscious and making it superconscious.

The Great Work on planet earth is to re-structure the ego, to, by transmuting ourselves, transmute the existing beliefs that haunt us and haunt this planet. We work and practice in order to pave the way for new experiences, using new *Words* based in trust. We are here to transmute the old beliefs—to transmute everything we have been taught that is centered in fear. We are here to re-wire our brains, re-wire our response to fear. We are here to transmute the tremendous fear thought forms that haunt our dreams and interfere with our creating a whole new bag of miracles and we are here to manifest cool beautiful dreams to guide our consciousness into a Brave New World. We are here to become the Philosopher's Stone through Love of Sophia until everything we touch turns to gold. This is possible and this is the Great Work and it *is* a Great Work.

CHAPTER THREE

LETTING GO; POLARITY; POWER POINTS AND THE LAW OF REVERSAL; CHOICELESS AND PATHLESS; PRACTICES AND PRAYER

*T*his *Seminar begins with someone asking "What does letting go really mean?"*

Letting go means *Nothing is Lost.* When you make the choice to be true to yourself it is the beginning of remembering Who You Are. You embark on a journey of transformation and discovery—of authentic Being—that requires you to let go of who you thought you were—this letting go happens in your deepest egoic agendas. Never be afraid that if you let go you lose something—the truth is that in this process of letting go, you gain your truth—your Authentic Self. Jesus said *"There is no profit in a man who gains the whole world and loses himself."* Letting go means letting go of attachment to the world of profit and gain and entering into a world of true wealth.

In this path of letting go and remembering, you are going to remember all the appropriate information about every major choice you have ever made—and this leads you to Who You Are—which is a place beyond choice—the choiceless choice—the pathless path—the glorious unknown.

As far as past lives are concerned, you know that I don't focus on past lives as being of any true significance. And I often wonder, when looking at past life chronicles, why is everyone Cleopatra or King Tut or someone of great spiritual or worldly accomplishment? What happens to the people who clean out the stables or act as cooks, cleaners, hair dressers and janitors?

And why is it true that you always have a significant past life with the beautiful people and not with the people who aren't celebrities of some sort or famous in some significant way? The whole past life arena seems fraught with ego traps. I was once asked in a private session if I could tell if that client had been an indigo child. That indigo child myth is a significant ego trap. It is actually creating more separation. And parents of indigo children are similar to parents who enter their children in beauty pageants. The truth is that we don't really know—we really don't know and why do we think we need to know? It is just another means of control.

Who can know what consciousness truly is and how it functions, lifetime after lifetime in this great universe? This is The Mystery of God. Science is trying hard to break the Mystery of God into usable fragments of information. Impossible—it is a Mystery. I pray that it can't be known. You are not going to ever forget your journey through the Mystery—for when all the questions are answered, we reach The Mystery and let go of questions forever. The human being is a monkey with a monkey-mind. When the monkey-mind is still, and there is no more obsession with interpreting the world because we have true knowledge, true Wisdom, then we can be the beautiful Mystery and revel in the wonder and wealth, the beauty and truth that is authentically present in each moment of our lives.

The ego is like a monkey protecting its little hoard of reality when all around it the majestic universe calls. We try to control letting go, like, *I have to control it so that I won't lose anything—if I let go I might lose something really important—I might lose my identity.*

Freedom requires that you let go of everything you thought was real so that Reality can come to you.

When you let go, you can't lose anything that is true to you, you can't lose Who You Are—at some level of consciousness you exist always, in a really vital way. Vital memories exist in the universe—this is why you so often find that when you are inspired, knowledge seems to come to you from out of nowhere and for want of a better word we call this *intuition*. But it is really that at some level, in the universal consciousness, vital knowledge and memories exist and we all tap into them. And this is where trust comes in—and this is why I say follow what's important to you; follow what catches your attention. If you run into a book and think it looks interesting, or if the proverbial book that falls off the shelf, falls on you, follow through, read it, pay attention to it because it is You calling to you, Self calling to self. This is why polarity is such an important principle, and utilizing power points is so important. In the practice of the Polarity Principle—in the space between points A and B is everything you already know. Meaning—you already know Who You Are.

Student: *"If the 'choiceless' choice and the 'pathless' path is our ultimate goal—then why do these practices in the Course emphasize choicework and Pathwork? How do we reach the 'pathless path' by practicing Pathwork? How do we become choiceless by practicing choice? It seems like a lot of contradictions—or deliberately misleading information."*

Another question might be why are people so often afraid of contradictions? This loops right back to control. It is in the way we are trained to think. Because the ego is always looking for certainty we are always looking for the *either/or* answer. Humans will debate for hours trying to arrive at a consensus, looking for an answer that creates a black and white outcome that resolves all contradictions. But really, there is no such thing as a contradiction—everything is contained within The Mystery. A contradiction has to do with our belief that we have to control the world. Contradiction simply means you are looking for an outcome that will define the world for you. If you know Who You Are in the world, there is no outcome that you will fear and you will not be afraid of contradictions. And there is no black and white—nature creates in technicolor and our relationship with nature is the Beauty of God made manifest.

In the Real Magic Course, choice and pathwork are only means of traveling. They contain no absolute truth. They have no power in themselves to create change. They are like Buddha's raft that takes you across the river and into the unknown. These practices are methods that allow you to traverse your own consciousness in a quest that follows a Divine Order—these methods of conscious choice and pathworking allow you to *stay conscious while you travel*. Pathwork *is* a pathless path. Choicework leads to the choiceless choice. Contemplate these truths. The keyword is conscious—be conscious of the choices you are making. Walk until you are always conscious of your Path.

Student: *"What about the outcome of war? Aren't there many contradictions there? Don't you have to defend yourself? Can you explain what power points mean in that context? If it is not too much review . . . ."*

As far as too much review goes . . . there is no such thing as too much review. If you've walked the Course ten times, you will still be reviewing. I review the teachings all the time—they are endlessly fascinating in the revelations they make possible.

War is not an outcome—it is a nightmare *process* that humans created believing it would solve problems. And war is a relationship—this is where choice comes in—your relationship with war is a choice you make—what kind of relationship do you want to have with war? Well, what are you willing to receive from war? For me, the answer is nothing. There is nothing that war has to offer me, nothing I can receive from war. For example, I do not believe that war is ever an answer—violence does not solve problems, it creates more problems. So since war exists as a reality in my life I have to take a stand about it, choose how to relate to it in each moment.

There are times when, if I see a violent action taking place in front of my eyes, I would stop it physically. There are times when I would support the people involved in conflict by staying out of it, not taking sides or trying to resolve it. The choice I make would depend on the energy of the moment. If I saw someone beating a child or an animal I would stop it. I have done so.

I would also—and do—create a mantra, a point B that declares and strengthens the quality of energy that I hope and pray will create the opposite of war in the world. My point B is empathy, compassion and truth.

Let's see . . . power points. Power points in the context of defending oneself. The concept of power points evolved for me as a teaching tool because when I first started teaching I found that I would have these moments in class where I would go blank, I would freeze, I wouldn't know what to do next and my ego would try to take over. I would be afraid. This was in the late 70s and except for Direct Guidance from the Christ Consciousness and my own highest intelligence, I did not have a teacher I could go to for help. At the time I was reading *"The Cloud of Unknowing"* by a Christian Mystic and I began to cultivate the art of *not knowing.* I would stop everything and inform the class that I had to stop because *I was afraid my ego was teaching the class—I was afraid of their pain, or afraid of them not getting it—so I would have to stop and take a moment to un-know and not know.*

This was a powerful teaching for me and for them. Because I was actually teaching, *"Don't be afraid of your ego, don't be afraid of being wrong, don't be afraid of any possible outcome, don't project outcomes, don't be afraid to be wrong."* It was around this time that I began naming those moments of fear as vital moments. I was not yet using the phrase "power point" but I was using moments of stress intuitively as points of letting go.

I had not yet intuited what to do with the information I'd received about *"vital moments."* But if I had reacted in an old way, of trying to save face and gain control over the moment, *I would have created a war* in the classroom because a collective ego-think would have taken over and my moment of fear would have become a "problem" and I would have tried to solve it by thinking in the old way and students would respond by challenging me, wanting to be right—they would respond by also thinking in the old way . . . and there would have been no space for wisdom.

In the old way of thinking—remember, Real Magic is focused on teaching you to think in a new way—we were taught to focus on fear, on outcomes, and on the anxiety about outcomes and on fixing or solving stressful moments. So we are habituated to holding on to intense anxiety when we are afraid of an outcome. This is a tremendous amount of attention we are cultivating around fear of outcomes. And what does attention create? Energy! And what does energy do? *It has to go somewhere*—energy always has to go somewhere, energy does things.

If your intention is all wrapped up in "I am afraid of what will happen!"—then what will happen is bound to be fearful because of that powerful focus. If you have no war in you as a potential outcome, your response to war will not be fearful—you will just be true—like Etty Hillesum or Sophie Scholl. They were both killed by the Nazi's—Sophie was beheaded as a traitor and Etty died in a concentration camp. In the midst of Nazi Germany they were unable to be anything but true to themselves. They were alive in their own goodness, their own intelligence and it was so alive in them that it was their constant Guidance. Etty said, *"I am God speaking and God listening."* Her fellow prisoners called her the speaking heart of the barracks and her simple courage and absolute commitment to truth was a source of inspiration for all who knew her; she even impacted some of her German guards, as did Sophie Scholl and the White Rose group. The effect that these people created by their compassion and fearless commitment to truth in the moment is still reverberating in the world.

So—in the ancient esoteric teachings, students were required to master stress, and a powerful moment of stress was called a *vital moment.* A vital moment was one of those split second shifts when your ego takes over and you go into a reality of threat, defense, fear, anger, grief, or pain. It is a moment of intensity, a moment when you feel so unsafe that you have to, at all costs and by any means necessary, bring yourself back to a safe place. It is a moment when you have to be right—all your programmed egoic strategies converge into making sure you are right. And this egoic definition of 'right' often means you subscribe to the status quo—you have to be right according to the prevailing definitions of "right" and your "righteousness" has to be recognized and validated by the world at large. And this usually means that you go to war.

All this split-second action happens in order that you can feel safe. In these vital moments, if you take charge and recognize that you are in a vital moment, you will have access to tremendous creative energies. There is a tremendous build up of energy in these moments.

In these vital moments, Mystery School students were taught to make use of something called The Law of Reversal. It is one of the innumerable esoteric Laws of Energy. The Law of Reversal simply tells you that you must reverse the flow of energy from point A (where you are at) to point B (what you are choosing to create). In this way you take this tremendous build up of creative energies and direct them away from Point A and toward Point B—this allows Creation to work in your behalf. This is the way to create something very new.

Student: *"Could you give an example?"*

It is very simple . . . your personality and daily existence is a program created by your beliefs, reactions, and thoughts about life, and in this programmed flow of yourself, all your attention and energy is normally focused toward maintaining your immediate, current state of reality. Everything in your current existence is focused—or you could say lives at—Point A. Point A contains the energy of your current state of reality and your own creative energy is locked into maintaining Point A—keeping that reality alive and well. Do you follow that? *(Several student's respond affirmatively)*

So when a belief state is activated within you and you feel threatened, and you recognize that you are in a power point, all the energy of your current state of reality is concentrated in that moment of stress—all of you is there in that stress energy of Point A. If you would like to transmute that energy of stress and transmute it into the energy of Freedom, it would behove you to know a practice that can gather all that stress energy and shift it—give it a huge shove—toward Freedom. The power point practice does just that. It teaches you to focus your attention in the moment and not stay in the haunted house of belief being terrorized by the energy of your past fear. It teaches you to reverse direction and shift from A to Point B. It is like putting money in the bank, you make a huge deposit of attention/energy at Point B.

The Law of Reversal states that if you are in a vital moment and you want to do something in that moment that will transmute your current existence, shifting the direction will be a powerful action toward transmuting Point A. As you practice this Law you come to understand that your most successful practice in that moment is to reverse the flow of your attention—shift it from an unconscious egoic attention into a conscious attention. Energetic shifts are always powerful moments because you can literally shift the energy in the direction you want it to go and you can feel that shift—this is an amazing feeling—that moment when you experience a shift within your own energy, and furthermore, a shift that you have consciously created, feels really powerful. This is worth working for.

So, when A gets energized and you realize you are in a power point, the Law of Reversal allows you to re-direct and focus the power of your attention toward the new point of attention at Point B. This focus on a creative *action* gives your mind something else to do, programs you to think in a new way, and releases you from having to think in a psychological way about what was energized. You simply take action to reverse your attention. The action of that reversal itself will create tremendous shift of focused energy toward Point B. The power of such vital creative energy focused on a *New Word* brings the new Word into being—the Word becomes flesh.

MECHANICS' INSTITUTE LIBRARY
57 Post Street
San Francisco, CA 94104
(415) 393-0101

So—a power point is a moment when you feel threatened and overwhelmed by the emotions called up in you by the activating of your belief clusters—all your buttons are wildly pushed. If you can claim the power of that moment, and say to yourself that you are in a power point, and *reverse* the energy, *reverse* the direction of your attention from A to B, you are claiming your creative power.

Once you are able to stop your headlong projection and call it a power point, you have come a long way toward mastering *being in the moment* and manifesting what you truly want *in that moment.*

Being in the moment is a marvelous spiritual cliché but hardly anyone has come up with an effective tool for actually practicing it. Well, our Hermetic ancestors came up with the tools—the Principle of Polarity and the practice of vital moments—Power Points—and the Law of Words of Power.

The Law of Reversal, the Principle of Polarity, Power Points and The Law of Definition and Words of Power are powerful practices that actually accelerate change. These are difficult practices to master because you are truly mastering the energy of the moment, mastering the art of focusing your attention in a moment when you are reacting intensely to stress and living in your past. You are actually shifting the energy of stress tension into the energy of creative tension.

It happens in a moment, a twinkling of an eye—you realize that you are in a vital moment, of vital power, vital creative energies—immense creative vitality is available to you—and you experience the shifting of energy. You can actually *feel* the shift in energy, feel it happen—and it feels amazing. It is a truly liberating practice—mastering the Moment.

Student: *"Can we talk about polarity? It seems a genius way to look at consciousness."*

Yes, I like to think that Creation, the Original Genius, came up with this principle and taught it to the First Teacher, who would have been the first Hermes Trismegistus. Polarity indicates two opposite poles. Polarity is a tool, a definition of two opposite realities which combined as opposites, create an energy map, a map of your own consciousness. This energy map represents actual realities—tangible realities that are operating in your life. This map is used in the process of transmutation. A polarity map gives you a visual of what energies are at play in your power points. It also gives you a structure—equivalent to *an alchemical vessel*—that contains and holds the creative energy you are working with—gathering and holding the energy and allowing it to build enough power to actually dissolve Point A and create new form at Point B.

The Principle of Polarity is a primary principle in the Hermetic Teachings. It is a primary practice for transmuting energy. You use the Principle of Polarity to create the visible map that you write as "Point A" and "Point B." *A—this is the existence I am in but do not want. I want to transmute Point A. And then you move right to the opposite pole, B—this is the existence I want to bring into being.*

This map represents the energy you are consciously choosing to work with.

Let me repeat this pattern. *As you practice these principles, you are using the Principle of Polarity to create the alchemical vessel that will hold the tremendous energies of Creation until the energies you have gathered actually work to transmute A and give form to B.*

Actually the true polarity is within yourself in the change from ego consciousness to truth consciousness. In the study of traditional, physical alchemy, the alchemist works with the material energies of the polarity—say you would collect metals, chemicals and mathematical formulas that represent point A then we take metals, chemicals and mathematical formulas that represent—all with the correct astrological correspondences—the other side of the polarity, point B, and we place them all in a vessel. The vessel represents the womb of Creation. Catalytic agents are added to the ingredients and the vessel is *hermetically* sealed. Heat is applied to the vessel and change happens within the vessel that transmutes the polarity from A into B—lead into gold.

In the Alchemy of the Soul, we work with metaphysical formulas and you are the vessel within which transmutation occurs and this visible map is a map that tells your *consciousness* which way you want it to go. The polarity map gives deliberate and powerful direction to your attention, your thoughts. You use it to reverse the direction of your attention so that your thoughts move in the direction of point B and stay focused there.

The Principle of Polarity is based on the understanding in the esoteric teachings of the principle of vibration. This principle states that everything that exists is a form of vibrating energy. Form itself is created from frequencies of vibration. A rock and a cloud are each given form by the frequency or rate of vibration within the form but a rock and a cloud are on different lines of polarity. A rock and a cloud are not opposites, they are different worlds—different vibratory worlds—therefore for our purposes they do not constitute a polarity.

In the Laws of Energy, a higher frequency of vibration will transmute a lower frequency if they are of the same *polarity*. For example: If they are both qualities, it is easy for the higher frequency to transmute the lower frequency. You can transmute subconscious to superconscious because they are polarized along the same line, and the superconscious is the highest quality, or frequency of vibration, a human being can aspire to. Therefore in the Principle of Vibration, Superconscious can transmute subconscious but subconscious cannot transmute Superconscious. But because the ego is guarding the content of the subconscious so that it won't change, once you make a choice to raise your vibration, your ego, which works energetically, senses the new, incoming vibration and goes into red alert, aware that a new and possibly dangerous outside other is entering your vibrational field. This is a bit of a Star Trek metaphor but it is accurate.

This means that what really gets transmuted in spiritual alchemy are the vibrational energies of emotions and qualities. Emotions and qualities are of the same polarity. You could say that anger and serenity are vibrating on the *same polarized line* but serenity is a higher frequency than anger so it can easily transmute anger. But a rose and an emotion, either anger or love, are different polarities therefore you cannot transmute anger into a rose—but you can transmute anger into serenity because they are on the same polarized line.

You can *compare* a rose to serenity if you are feeling poetic. And this will energize your movement toward actual serenity. You can say the rose makes you feel serene and you can use the rose as a creative tool to help you displace, reverse, and transmute your feelings of anger. You can even use the white rose to represent the Feminine Christ Consciousness—Sophia. (This is why the White Rose is the Real Magic logos.) But you cannot change the actual cellular frequency of a rose into an actual quality like anger because they are not on the same line and can't be polarized.

To recapitulate, you can start with fear and transmute it to fearless by first creating a polarity map of what you want your consciousness to do—at Point A you write: Fear; at Point B you write: Fearless. Then you work with that map by creating mantras and utilizing power points. It really is that simple. What you are doing in a power point is energizing the polarity, taking all the energy and allowing it to *dissipate* around point A *(breaking the ego loop)* and simultaneously allowing tremendous, fresh, new, energy to build around point B. If you can focus your attention, especially in a power point, you are going to be successful. But this is a rigorous practice—at first it can feel like patting your head and rubbing your stomach at the same time.

Student: *"I have been thinking of the word intention. In a Power Point what we do at point B is focus attention on an intention that is specific to the moment. The polarity to anger might be joy for you, in a specific moment."*

Oh yes. And it might be peace in another instance, or compassion, understanding, or wisdom. It can shift to ecstasy—there are no rigid rules about polarities. The basic rule of transmuting energy or manifesting anything is that there be a strong and clear intention to focus on at point B. But that intention can be specific to you and have to do with the ways in which you define words.

Student: *"What about humor"*

Oh yes, humor is always good. Humor that is not mockery is of a high vibration. Humor is a choice you can make in response to a situation. It is the opposite of humorless, taking things too personally can change to seeing the humor, the absurd, in your own responses to experience. Such humor can help you take your self-importance and transmute it into wisdom.

Student: *"What are some of the things you talk about to recognize when you're in a power point?*

Another Student: *"Well, I think you started at the beginning where you have that feeling that you're threatened or you feel like you need to be in control. It's that stress. I know that a lot of my power points came from this very strong internal, constant voice about what I was doing right or wrong and I started to start recognizing that as a power point. This created much more space. I was thinking about how in a power point, when you are able to start recognizing it, it's like you're taking yourself back to the power of choice."*

Yes. When you are most stressed! You have a choice in that moment to transmute stress.

Student: *"And when you're most stressed, that's when you are most unconscious."*

Absolutely. Stress is unconsciousness. It is good to notice that when you are in a power point you have the opportunity to take a part of you that is unconscious and make it conscious. You are lost in the trash—what do you want?—treasure! You are asleep on your feet—what do you want?—to wake up! You are locked into beliefs about the lumps of coal—loss and lack—in your life—what do you want?—diamonds! Curse or Blessing?

Student: *"Victim to Freedom."*

Yes, thank you. Freedom.

Student: *"The more that I've done this the better I feel all the time. So when it comes up it's really glaringly obvious like: Wow, I don't like this. But when you were talking about practices, I wondered, do I do practices? I don't think what I do is practice"*

Yes—even masters are spiritual practitioners. You are thinking of practice as a verb. A spiritual practice is actually a noun. The verb/noun would be "you should *practice* your spiritual *practices*".

Same Student: (interrupting) *"But I don't feel like I'm practicing. I realize, or become aware that I'm starting to feel real funky and I don't like feeling really funky, whatever it is, fear or anger or whatever. So I immediately change the focus."*

Then, yes, you are doing a spiritual practice—you just described a spiritual practice. You are practicing your spiritual practices! That makes you a spiritual practitioner.

You are in confusion about what a practice is and you are defining *practice* in an egocentric way. In the eyes of your ego, to be just practicing means you are just an amateur. In a psycho/linear world when you practice something you are focused on *process* and you are focused on an *outcome*. In this case—say you are practicing for a piano recital or a sports event—the practice is about a projected outcome, a goal, and there are a lot of egocentric energies involved, such as the energy of competition. In this case to say you are practicing means you are *just* practicing, which of course, means you are just a beginner, just an amateur.

A spiritual practitioner, on the other hand, is *always practicing* and there is no competition (or if there is it becomes a painful lesson) and no outcome to focus on—because the practices are about Who You Are. Spiritual practices are *not debatable!* "Do your practices" is like a command from a Divine Source. A spiritual practice is its own reward. The essence of spiritual practice is the recognition that you are always practicing—in the moment—and that you are practicing being who you are; being true to yourself.

Your ego doesn't like the word *practice* because it makes you sound like a beginner and you prefer to think of yourself as an adept—a successful student, even a master—who no longer needs to practice. This is your competitive ego *in practice (student laughter)!*

If you practice your spiritual practices in a constant way, shifts begin to happen automatically. You can define yourself as a master, if you like, but until you know, in your total being, *who you are,* you are a practitioner—and when you know who you are, you are still a practitioner. I am a constant practitioner, a constant gardener, creating compost, digging up toxic weeds, allowing beauty and grace to grow. This is my practice. This is my constancy and the challenge with this is to be a constant practitioner without focusing on process or outcome.

Student: *"And the reward is being in a situation where you see yourself completely naturally respond to something that previously would have been devastating. This is so cool".*

Yes.

Student: *"One of the ways you explained to me that helped me remember power points is you described it simply as a moment of intense emotion. The reason that worked for me is because I know that intense emotion can be angry or stressed or scared. So when I'm in intense emotion, I know I'm in a power point."*

Thank you. The negative emotion in a power point is intense and overwhelming. And in a moment—in the twinkling of an eye—the frequency of rage/pain/fear can become the emotion of serenity which can be *just as intense* in a different way—without the self-importance—a blessing way.

There is a passage in the Christian Bible that goes, *"In a moment, in the twinkling of an eye; we shall all be changed."* That phrase hit me when I was a child and I have always loved that concept of change happening in the twinkling of an eye. And this can become a way of life, to transmute in the moment, any negative or destructive emotion that arises within you.

Negative emotion is such a deeply programmed reaction that it becomes an uncontrollable reaction. So don't try to control it. You are in it before you know it, it's not as if you've made a choice and said to yourself, *oh, I think I'll have a power point.* When you are in an unconscious state of being, you just react. This moment—when you go unconscious—is the moment when you *practice recognizing* that you are in a vital moment. Then you can say, Stop! And reverse the direction. People create deliberate and helpful physical signals to themselves that they use in these vital moments. Some people look up with their eyes.

Student: *"God help me."* (student laughter)

Yes, God help me, or go down on your knees! It is a powerful shift that you begin to recognize—you can actually begin to feel it shift—and that is very rewarding. And doing a physical movement with your eyes or your hands helps get the flow of energy going—some gesture that says that you want to reverse the energy. Like a gesture with your thumb toward the direction you want to go—a cosmic hitchhiker.

Yes, it is like you take your attention off of *here*, the victim, and shift it to *here*, the Blessing. And as you practice this over and over, repeat it over and over, you begin to recognize the energy shift when it happens.

Student: *"The other thing that works for me that you explained a long time ago is that when you're in that intense emotion and when you realize what it is that's causing it, to think of the opposite. Like, so, what is point A and then go to the opposite of the point A emotion. That way I know that I'm redirecting my attention away from and not toward the way I'm feeling right now, For me that's about focusing and taking my attention off of what's not working for me."*

Yes, you are talking about the Principle of Polarity—that creating the polarity, opposite poles, A and B—these are two *opposite intentions*—gives you a visible, tangible, map of what you want your attention to do—so that when you are in stress and remember that you have a map, you can *learn to remember* that you want your attention to be focused on B. The significance of A and B is they are *opposite intentions*—such as fear and fearless. Or trash and treasure. Coal and diamond. Curse and blessing. Anger or peace.

By practicing the Principle of Polarity, you find what works best for you in power points because you are working with opposite intentions. You *practice* the quality you want most to be, to embody as a constant state within you. Like Grace. I used that all the time . . . every time I was in a power point it was: *Grace*. Or Peace, Blessing, or Wisdom.

Student: *"Could you tell us the story about 9-11? The peace in the tress . . ."*

Yes, it was an amazing blessed experience—at one of our worst collective planetary moments I was able to realize Peace. On Sept. 11, 2001, my phone rang at, I think it was, between 8 and 9 in the morning. It was my son in Seattle telling me to turn on my TV. And as I watched the second attack on the towers and the heart-wrenching images, my first instantaneous insight was, *"Well, Bush has got his war!"* It was a sad realization of everything implied in those images and all my knowing about President Bush and the current administration. So my second realization came immediately and automatically, I went right to *Peace*. I thought: peace—this has got to be about peace. Then my phone started ringing. Many, many, people were calling, horrified and very frightened by the event.

Finally, in the afternoon, I felt exhausted. I turned the phone off and went outside and sat on my back deck steps, wanting to breathe with nature and quiet my mind and breathe peace into my heart. I started breathing peace and all of a sudden I became aware that Peace itself was *pulsing—emanating from—*the trees and the grass and my entire garden, even the huge fir and cottonwood trees, even the air and clouds, were pulsing, breathing, emanating a great Peace. I said "Oh my God!" and I just let go into weeping.

I sat on the steps and surrendered into it, just went *into* it and I felt all the people who had been so shocked in that moment the planes hit, felt the ones who had turned and began praying for peace. So many people had focused on peace that it was emanating from the planet. This amazing focus, this prayer for peace was so amazing—it was pulsing—a *great pulse*, animals, trees, the grass, the water, the rocks, *mountains*, were pulsing peace because that response had been created in so many of us, all of us who have been working for change all our lives, had spent so many years practicing and choosing peace that we could now emanate, in this tremendous, vital moment, *the thing we truly wanted.*

It was so powerful. It was the most powerful thing I have ever experienced, that pulsing peace of the earth. It was utterly real, it was the earth's response to human madness because enough people . . . enough of *us* . . . have faith in the Great Work, faith in the earth and Her ability to resonate with us, enough of us have faith in peace, we were emanating that frequency and the earth was expressing it. It's real, it is *real*. Don't ever stop praying for peace because it is real. In the face of everything, go to Peace. Make it real, again and again, make it real. Point B is manifest Peace.

Student: *"What about when you think about someone you know who has cancer, a child, can you reverse that . . . ?"*

No, *you* cannot reverse that . . . . But you can assist them to reverse it themselves if they choose to.

Another Student: *". . . then. how do you pray for someone? Because you are projecting unless they asked you to pray for something specific for them . . . right?"*

Not necessarily—that is too judgmental. Remember, *intention is everything.* For you to try to judge or reverse another person's reality is a manipulation, and manipulation is always wrong because it is wrong to interfere with their choice or pretend to know what their choice is or should be. Trying to take their choice away from them—that is a projection—trying to make them choose what you want them to receive.

But you can offer them a prayer that supports their choice and ask that your prayer be appropriate. There is a difference between praying for someone and trying to make their choices for them. You cannot create for anyone but yourself. Choice is the energy of free will, it is a very real energy and very individual. The best thing you can do for others is to become a conscious being.

A prayer is simple, you are not projecting, you are *communing.* Prayer comes from your sincere desire to comfort and assist, not a desire to take control, but a desire that health, peace, compassion, and wisdom *be available* in the world for this person. Pray like a child—"please God please help mommy or daddy or sister or my puppy, or kitten, or Uncle Bob—and show me how I can help them." I prayed that way when I was a child. I once wanted to pray for someone who had died and a relative told me I couldn't pray for dead people—but I prayed anyway—and I saw, had a vision of that person safe in the arms of Jesus. That vision made me very happy.

With that kind of intention there is no "me, me, me . . ." in it. Everything is, of course, all about intention. Pray to God, or to the Source, or to the Source of Grace, or to Creation—God is a vast Intention—all those phrases refer to a vast and unmistakable Intelligence and Grace and the Cosmic Intention that is in all our cells.

Student: *"Didn't you tell a story about a traffic accident where someone died and some people in their cars were held up and were looking at their watches and cursing and one person sent light and love . . . ."*

Another Student: *"There was a car accident and there was a woman in the line of traffic behind who actively started praying for the person who had been injured in the accident, and . . . she didn't die and she remembered the energy of the prayer."*

Another Student: *"I heard this story told on Maui as if it had happened there . . . I heard that she had left her body, like maybe a near death experience, in the accident, and then was taken to the hospital and recovered after a long period of time. When she had left her body she was able to see the different responses of the people in the line of traffic behind the accident—like, "shoot, I'm going to be late, or damn this always happens along this stretch of road", and then she noticed the woman who was praying for her, the woman was praying "Please give her peace and help her". She noticed the license plate on the car and when she got better and was out of the hospital she looked up the woman who had prayed for her and went to her and thanked her."*

Yes, that is a lovely true story. Prayer is so often associated with miracles. It has great power to make a difference—and it cannot be analyzed, that is the beauty of it.

Student: *"My questions came up because you asked us in an email to pray for _____ whom I have never met. It started me thinking about how many people in the world are suffering severely and I thought, where do you stop? Or where do you start? Or just say: May all beings have peace, may all beings have happiness, and leave it at that. Or if I start naming people . . . ?"*

Yes, there is the Buddhist metta prayer, and the metta prayer is a beautiful prayer—may all beings have peace . . . this is always a good prayer. So you are asking where do you start and stop? You begin with your heart and you never stop. But you let go of any anxiety or dread about the prayer. Let go of outcomes—let go of anxiety and go to Faith. You can pray for anything anytime—all the time. It really doesn't matter because it is the intention within you that matters; it is your compassion that matters. Prayer is different from meditation but they all serve the purpose of focusing Light. When you are meditating you are focused and when you focus, you receive, and merge with the Source of Light.

Prayer is the act of *petitioning* the Source, it doesn't require a powerful focus, or even a clear consciousness—you just say "please." There is gratitude in prayer, a humility before the power of Grace. You might be praying to a deity, to a Presence, a Higher Power, asking that Higher Power to make a difference—the words don't matter, the intention works. There are studies now, studying prayer and the fact that it works. So don't try and figure or control the "how" of prayer—just say *please*. For instance the prayer I asked you to do for _____ was a simple "please help her to receive whatever Light she needs, and help her to feel peace."

And whichever one you choose, prayer or meditation, both are very powerful because intention is the most powerful force in the universe. Imagine intention sent forth and gathering energy and then focusing that energy . . . we make more Light available . . . yes, pray for Light to be available.

Student: *"What about people who aren't choosing peace . . . they like anger."*

Well, do you *know* if they *"like"* anger? Does anyone *like* anger? I think you mean that some people unconsciously choose anger because feel more powerful when they are angry and they become addicted to anger because of this. Some people believe that anger is too powerful to change. But does that mean they *like* anger?

Don't pray for anyone or anything if there is any doubt in you—you cannot control prayer—and don't pray if you feel anything of judgment or anger for the person—pray for *yourself* in that case. Pray for the compassion or Grace that will help you let go of your judgments and conditions. Don't pray for peace for them, pray for yourself, ask to receive Peace, all the Light—ask that the loving and unconditional Source be available to you and them. Don't say, heal so-and-so's cancer, say, instead, give so-and-so whatever she needs most. Don't say heal so-and-so's anger. Say, thank you, God. Help me transmute any anger in me and give so-and-so whatever they need most. May all being have peace.

Student: *"I sometimes say, 'give them peace and courage . . . ."*

Yes, basic qualities. The intelligent universe that we live in is so intelligent it will give us what we need and there is no them, or they, in this Intelligent Eye. Sometimes when I ask for Guidance about any of this I receive a sense of be *still.* Be still. Be still. And stay still.

Sometimes the worst thing we can do is stay upset about another person's situation or emotions. It is theirs. Let them have it. Do not get into it with them. Do not feed their fear. Sometimes your most well-meant words or actions just feed their ego. Do not feed the ego—that would be a good slogan on t-shirts. *Do not feed the ego. Just create peace.*

Sometimes a well-meaning action on your part will delay or interrupt something that they need to experience. Or their own choices will somehow subvert your good action. When I worked as a hands-on energetic, healer, I would work with someone and do a lot of healing and they would leave feeling refreshed and healed, feeling no pain, able to use their legs again, and that sort of thing. Then they would come back in weeks or months and the pain or trauma would have moved from their shoulder to their hips, or from their knees to their back. They had brought it back—the same trauma but in a new form—*because they had not chosen to release it!*

I had been studying Esoteric systems and I was continually receiving the Guidance to teach people *how* to let go of ego and transmute energy so that they themselves could make their own changes. So I began teaching people how to work with energy, how to make conscious choices, what choice is, how to think in a new way about it, that it is the choices they make that creates the transmutation they want. In other words, how to free themselves and not depend on anyone for their freedom.

I remember one man in particular. He was a Vietnam Vet and had been wounded in the shoulder and neck. He had a trachea tube and was intensely depressed and anguished, and as I worked with him I realized that he had a tremendous guilt and a bad case of self-hate. I worked with him for a couple of years and he was quite improved in his outlook on life and was in much more peace when he left the area. While I worked with him he went through many experiences of his agony moving around within his body—I remember at one point it moved into his knees and lower leg and he couldn't walk. We worked through each point in his process and I learned so much from him.

He left town and so did I and I didn't see him for years. The last time I saw him we were both visiting the town we had lived in and he was married—and this was big because he had carried a huge and very alive thought form of belief that his injuries would prevent anyone from loving him. He told me how after he'd met the woman who became his wife, he had had a huge healing crisis, laying on the floor crying, and it suddenly came to him that he was just a kid, just a boy when he was in Vietnam, and that he had not invented war or created Vietnam. He said he was lying on the floor yelling that it wasn't his fault that war existed. And he also let go of his guilt that he had lived and so many of his buddies had died. So, as he forgave himself, he suddenly experienced who he really was and became a peace maker because so much peace poured into him as he had those revelations and he let go of guilt and self-condemnation in one swoop.

Student: *"I was just thinking about healing. There are so many people who are able to get healing, like Reiki and energetic healings. A lot of times it works but a lot of times it comes back in some form."*

Yes, it seems like many factors are involved in each individual healing—but essentially it all boils down to the deep and hidden intentions within the individual. There is no such thing as healing . . . really. There is only being true to yourself . . . and you can't really make any kind of broad statement about healing. And you can't make any claims . . . you can only do your best to be in touch with what you want to transmute and the fact that you actually *do want* to transmute your dark side. It is about many factors that all have to do with lifetimes of choices and intentions within each person. Because wholeness is an individual thing, and choices and creating . . . that's different with each individual. I had one man who, when he walked in. said he wanted to be a medical miracle, and when I was working on him I saw how real that was to him so I was able to say to him that he was already a medical miracle—and he was. He had a miraculous heart healing and it was real and lasting.

Now another person might say they want to be a medical miracle and the miracle won't manifest because there is just too much fear in them—and the fear is constantly debating and interfering with the miracle and attracting more fear. Another person might say they want to be a medical miracle and they die, but they will die happy and in peace, because that's what they really, really wanted—to be in peace and not be afraid of death.

There is so much that we just don't know—and that is why it is best to have no assumptions about anything or anyone—and don't ever condemn ourselves.

Student: *"I am thinking about Krishnamurti and his problems with his health . . . so many spiritual teachers have strong health problems . . . why do we make such a big deal of this?"*

Yes . . . that did not mean K was not a great teacher—or that teachers have to be perfectly healthy. Most of them aren't. Everyone has to die, it is part of the cycle of earthly life. It seems that today there are many young teachers who are into fitness and studying alternative healing technologies and they have a lot of fear and judgments about illness. But I imagine that we all come eventually to the understanding that the only healing is self-knowledge—*know thyself* is our purpose for being here on earth.

Many spiritual teachers go through life with health problems—it doesn't mean anything—they work hard—they work as transmuters and they work with enormous amounts of energy—and they tend to ignore their own health—maybe they are tired—that's all it means. The first time I went to a healer—it was in 1972—I felt kind of ridiculous because I had never done anything like that and she told me I was always going to have trouble with my lungs because I have so much collective grief stored in them that I had forgotten how to breathe. I went, *"Oh yeah—right!"* but shortly after that I was diagnosed with emphysema. I experienced a miraculous healing with that—but breathing and asthma and allergies are still a key factor in my health. And many, many spiritual teachers have diabetes—what's up with that? Diabetes is a disorder within the center of transformation. Maybe they just don't have time to release all the energy they are transmuting. Maybe that is all it is—just what is.

Many spiritual teachers feed the myth of perfection by not allowing any publicity about their physical afflictions—and their core group protects them—keeps it from becoming known that the teacher is unwell. Again I say, what's up with that? Why are we supposed to be perfect? I very deliberately share my process with my students and expose my imperfections simply as a protest against the myth of spiritual teachers having to be perfect. You have to ask, "Perfect as defined by whom?" Who defines perfect? Too often it is ego that is defining what perfect means.

So who knows—God is a beautiful mystery that never needs fixing. And maybe a spiritual teacher is a beautiful mystery that doesn't need fixing—that's what I feel about my own health. Who knows what is really going on anywhere, anytime? We can only know our choices, our piece of it, our own awareness within the world we inhabit. And being aware within the world means knowing Who You Are.

Student: *"We were going to talk about the subtleties of victim."*

We were? *(student laugher)* I'm sorry if I got distracted. I do that.

Okay. Victim—Intention is everything and we all carry beliefs about who we are and what the world is and what we ought to be and what the world ought to be—*each of these beliefs acts as an intention.* So a victim belief system holds us to the intention to feel an identity of victim and we will manifest various forms of victim. This is a very subtle action of the ego. What did you want to say about victim? About the subtleties . . . ?

Student: *"Yes. In the story that I had made reference to earlier about the email that you sent me [*I believe what she is referring to is actually on a different tape] *I'd been tootin' along doing really well. Then my daughter left home and she was 3,000 miles away and it was fine and we have a great relationship. We're very independent and I love my solitude, but it was a big hit not to have her there anymore. So I went through some grieving and that's fine, but I saw that the body was responding really severely because the mother/child connection is so strong. I noticed that it triggered into . . . okay . . . the man that I've been seeing for years hasn't been there to be supportive and I have other friends that are saying, "Oh didn't he call you? Isn't he there to support you because your daughter just left?" And, "How are you doing with your daughter gone?" . . . . and all this. These were well meaning friends, who are pretty aware, and it fed and triggered my little victim. Then I'm thinking. "Why isn't he calling me? Where is my support?" So I emailed you and you emailed back oh my God . . . ."* (long pause)

What?

Student: *"The point is that it wasn't like a huge victim that was really obvious to everybody, and well-meaning friends saying . . . "Oh how are you doing . . . your daughter's gone . . ." But there's this sense that he should be doing this or that or that I should be feeling this or that. Then getting the reality check of Truth from Sylvia . . . you even said something like his only responsibility is to be true to himself . . . then it was like . . . boom, I let it all go."*

Probably I said "Is he responsible for your well-being?" When we are true to ourselves, empathy is part of our nature, part of that. But empathy and compassion don't mean that we feed each other's victim—and true well-being might mean that we don't encourage self-pity. The subtlety of victim is that we tend to make other people responsible for our well-being—they are supposed to make us feel better, take care of us.

It is very subtle. This unconscious action of the ego . . . when the energy goes unconscious, everyone gets enlisted in the story, involved in the action. This is actually a very subtle power point . . . .

This subtlety—this story about the daughter leaving illustrates the subtlety of the collective ego, working with *agreed upon* states of being. Did anyone say,

"Your daughter is leaving, Congratulations! Let us raise a toast to both of you and your passage through life!"

No, that was not the agreed upon story. The subtlety of victim is that you don't realize that it is *just a story and not even a true story*, a choice you made long ago to agree to look at things in a certain way and to believe certain things about reality—and this choice/belief/agreement colored all your thinking and your actions. You think it is real. But is it real? No, it is just a story that many people have agreed to believe in.

The agreed upon story between friends—because this is what friends do—agree upon who, what, how, and where . . . what to believe, what is required in the energy of "friendship"—and friendship is a story that two or more people are creating—and the agreed upon story in this case is very often, *"Oh, your daughters gone . . . you must be feeling lonely . . . sad and lost."* This story is creating a melodrama, a stage setting for the feelings of fear that this brings up in the friends involved. Why are they fearful? Because they are involved in their own stories which are triggered by this agreed upon story of your damage—your loneliness and loss. Which they are assuming and projecting. People believe that they have to react with sympathy, but why? This is life. This is truth. Why must it be a cause for melodrama?

Why is there anything to fix? Your daughter is gone. You feel many feelings and these feelings are natural. Let the feelings be. Don't tell yourself stories about the feelings. Feel and respect what you feel but do not perpetuate it by involving you and your daughter in a story. A feeling of loneliness and sadness will pass on its own because it is simply the ego's fear of being alone, of abandonment, of not being in control of a situation. Don't cling, only the ego clings, the Spirit is Free.

Why do people believe that this feeling of victim indicates that someone owes us something? We are taught this—that the world owes us—and it is awful. Why does the boyfriend owe you sympathy and attention? Why is this, your child's passage, not a cause for rejoicing—to have a child pass through into a greater life? To have a child who is on a path that *you can't control* but which will bring them into knowing who they are—or maybe it won't but whatever life brings them will be theirs and you will have a whole new world of life to share with them, a whole new level of communication and maturity. Rejoice in that, pray for them, feel sad, miss them, long to see them, but do not allow fear to create a story. This is something to rejoice in.

Believe me I know. I have run the gamut of children leaving, children messing up, children making strange choices (that means choices that I couldn't understand!) and me messing up many, many times, trying to influence the choices they make, and finally arriving at having to be still and let them be and let myself be because they are not me or mine, I do not possess them, I love them.

You walk through a every kind of feeling and arrive at the simple joy of knowing them, of having them bless your life—even when they irritate you, even when they break your heart, the truth is a simple joy in being alive at this same moment in time with them.

So don't let your fear collide with theirs and don't let their fear disturb your peace. And don't let your fear disturb theirs. Neither of you is a victim. Don't perpetuate fear stories. Victim is just an agreed upon story, just a point of view that has to do with blame (someone is to blame) that you have agreed to act out and believe. It is not real or true. Choose to rejoice—you and your children chose to walk a path of Love on this beautiful planet, to be together, for a moment together, in this world, for the great privilege of loving. In this way we will heal wounded love, and heal wounded lives. This is Truth. Celebrate this. *"And we are put on earth a little space, that we may learn to bear the beams of Love."* (William Blake)

CHAPTER FOUR

MEDITATION; DANGER; COMPASSION; BELIEFS; DRAMA

This Seminar Opened With a Guided Meditation:

. . . Just close your eyes and feel your life. What is your life? How does it feel? Does your life consist of all your thoughts about things you believe that you are owed in life, the things you lack, things the world owes to you? The ways the world has damaged you? Or is your life focused on creating a new Book of You, of agreements and promises based on self-knowledge, on true choice, on who you really are, on the existence you really want to create. You are here, now, in this world. You are here in this world for just a moment. What do you want to create for your moment in this world?

Make an agreement. Agree to this—that there will be nothing in your new book based on obligation or fear about the past or future, let go of the past and the future and in your heart see yourself and your life as new and renewed—a new beginning for a new existence.

See yourself as at a new starting point based on what you want in the deepest and truest heart of your Self. Begin to breathe radiance, radiant Light, breathe it into your life. Your life is just beginning. There's nothing you have to finish. There are no conditions. There are no false agreements or promises made from fear. You are in a new beginning of radical, radiant love . . . a new beginning . . . nothing damaging or negative attached. All old stories about victim and lack are gone.

Your life is your birthright. It is yours free and clear. It is about Love. A Love you don't have to earn. You don't have to compete for it. There is nothing you have to be or do . . . nothing you have to agree to or promise before you can receive Love. And . . . there is nothing you can do to destroy it. This Love is yours . . . unconditionally . . . . Breathe that . . . . Take some deep, deep breaths, relax into the breath. Relax into Love. Fall into Light. Relax.

Now . . . Open your eyes and be present . . . and stretch . . . .

There you are. You are bathed in radiant, unconditional love, ready to become a new existence. What happens? What gets in the way? What creates the biggest obstacles to your freedom? Beliefs. Human beings are beings who live by belief. Anything that we experience, that we tell ourselves is true will become a belief.

Beliefs are very personal, they come from emotional certainties, and they're also collective. There are collectively agreed upon beliefs in this world that are dangerous to life. Like the bottom line human belief—somebody tell me the bottom line belief that lives in the human ego—the most dangerous belief we carry—what is it?

Students yell: *"Dangerous Others!"*

Dangerous others—that we live in a world that is dangerous—that we live in a world full of potentially dangerous others and that we won't be safe until all of these dangerous others are be *on our side*, to either share our beliefs—or to be controlled or killed. There's no possibility of debate in the ego about dangerous others. And that belief is in each one of us. It's a cellular belief. It's in our brain cells, in our brain chemistry; it's in all of our cells, in our guts and in our hearts. Fortunately for the human species, this can be transmuted—we have the ability to transcend and transmute our most dangerous beliefs.

Student: *"I have a question about that. What about the people in Iraq—that kind of thing—who are tortured by their government—and stuff like that?"*

Well, I am assuming that you are here in this Course because you want to change all that. All human beings wherever they are living have the ability to transmute energy and live in a state of Truth and Peace. No matter what or where. I don't know if I would have that much courage—to exist as love while in a place of torture, fear, and mockery. But look at some of our greatest heroes—Etty Hillisum who died in a concentration camp but refused to allow the Nazis to turn her into a victim—look at Sophie Scholl and her brother Hans, imprisoned and beheaded by the Nazis because they would not retract their passion for truth, their love and their belief that freedom is the birthright of all people.

Student: *"But . . . It's like they're actually living in danger it seems."*

And we aren't? Look at the way you are defining danger—from the point of view of fear, of ego. You are in danger right now. You are defining danger in a survivalist egocentric mode. Do you believe you are not living in danger simply because you are not being physically tortured and your country is not being invaded by dangerous soldiers from another country? What about the kid down the street who is being tortured daily by his parents? Danger to what? *Danger of what?* If danger exists as a concept, we are all living in it.

So—right, they are in physical danger and we are all in danger of being crippled or tortured or killed. Living in danger comes from being afraid of death and therefore danger is just as much illusion as death. So what is living in danger? Why are we so afraid of the fact that this body can die, that this body can be damaged is terrifying, that we can be damaged by this dangerous life . . . why is that terrifying? Are there degrees of danger? Is some danger worse than others? Does the Soul distinguish one death from another? Is any danger worse than the fear of danger?

In a beautiful statement about an imprisoned friend of his, the Dalai Lama tells us that there is a worse danger than the physical—the danger of becoming cynical, of losing our courage, of losing our desire to help the world, of learning hate, of losing our empathy, of losing our capacity for compassion.

It is a great wrong that any being has to live in the fear of torture and death—and that others can be complacent in the face of such suffering is wrong. But isn't it also wrong to perpetuate the belief that only physical danger is real? The belief that there are degrees of danger and some danger is worse than others is an illusion. That danger is *real* is an illusion. The Soul cannot be subject to danger—there is no such thing in the life of the Soul. The Soul is Light incarnate.

Are you asking if I feel compassion for them and would stop their torture if it was happening in my presence? Of course I feel compassion and would stop it. But everything I do, every class I teach, every breath I take is because I believe that the prevailing beliefs on this planet can be transmuted—can be stopped—*has* to be stopped. But I do not believe they can be stopped through fear, violence, and war.

But what is the real question?—*why* are these particular people living in physical danger? What is the true reason? They are in physical danger because of a bottom line belief on this planet. A belief in dangerous others. A belief in Us vs. Them. A belief that separation is healthy. A belief that war or violence can solve problems. A belief in scapegoating. A belief in the reality of lack. *That* belief means anyone who's in your way or who has something you want or need can be defined as a dangerous other and you and anyone you can enlist *on your side* in that belief have permission to destroy the dangerous other—the Blacks, the Jews, the Iraqi's, the people next door, your wife, your husband, your child—any number of dangerous, dangerous others exist, are there to be defined and blamed and controlled by torture and the fear of death—destroyed. There is only one rule in the kingdom of dangerous others and this rule holds true no matter who or what that dangerous other is—change them or destroy them.

Iraq is happening because human beings believe in dangerous others. Iraq is happening because of the human belief that fear is *real, that torture is real, dangerous others are real, and blame is real.* Iraq is happening because the human ego is full of fear, of self important beliefs, beliefs that give us permission to define Iraq as a dangerous other and declare *"If it's a dangerous other I have the right to either control it, or destroy it."*

And of all the fears that drive us, the fear of lack, of having to do without, of starving, of hunger that cannot be assuaged, is the most awful.

And there is no debate about this. Most humans would agree with this, whether they are from Iraq or United States.

Most war is economic—is about resources—whether it is oil, land, gold, water, or religious resources, human beings are functioning from a deep fear of lack, belief in damage, and belief in dangerous others.

Student: *"What about the proverbial dangerous other who tries to hurt or destroy a loved one? Would you stop them?"*

I have no idea what I would do. Certainly I would do something but I do not know what I would do until, and unless, it was happening—that is much too theoretical. I can only trust that in the moment I would know what to do because I would be true to myself. If one of my children—or any child—or a dog in the street—was in danger of torture and death I would take action. But taking action in the face of violence does not have to be a violent reaction. I would ask for Grace. I would ask the Source of Grace for help. What can I create that will change this? It would be a moment of truth. I know that I wouldn't hesitate to give my life and go with Grace in the face of violence. I would have the courage to be that true to myself. If I could do nothing else, I would offer up my life to shift things, to change the energy. But rather than be that melodramatic, I would rather be constant in my faith and trust my Authentic Self and not create that kind of illusion for myself or my children.

I had a shocking experience with belief when someone that I knew pretty well told me (in 2004) that he was going to vote for Bush because Bush will keep the military strong and will keep the war with Iraq going and he feels safer with Bush keeping that war going. This was a real challenge for me.

Student: *"That was his ego talking isn't it?"*

Well, yes it was his fear talking, certainly, but this is not about judging whether he was his ego. To be accurate it was his belief talking. And it was the whole political machine talking, the whole military/industrial complex and the desire for safety. My friend is a good person and he truly believed that we need a strong military. I had to let him be. There was no way I could conflict—go to war—with him about what he believes—I let him be, knowing, well, yes, what do we know? Maybe it—the sorrow and challenge I felt—was all about my beliefs.

Student: *"Because it activated you on some level?"*

Yes—what do I know? All I knew at the moment was that I was not willing to fight with him—or to be accurate I was not willing to *hurt* him—over the fact that he doesn't share my beliefs. I might wish he shared my beliefs—but he doesn't.

Maybe it activated me because I have a deep belief in these Hermetic teachings—that if everyone knew and practiced these teachings, we could save the world and maybe there is a hidden fear in me that it—these teachings and my faith in them—is a lie, maybe they have no power. Maybe there is nothing that will save the world! Maybe it is all hopeless. Maybe I have a hidden fear that these teachings are not enough—that maybe nothing has enough power to change the human ego.

So what do we do? What do we do as human beings? We can say, "Oh, that's about *their* beliefs and that's about *their* survival." But at some point you have to say, *"What is it about for me?"* Well it is *always* about what I want. I want Peace. I want Love, Compassion, Wisdom. Even if it never happens, I want unconditional wisdom on planet Earth and I am willing to give my life to that. Even if I never see it happen, I want this planet to be a source of wisdom, for all beings. But most of all, more than anything, personally, I want to be compassionate—for real.

You have to realize that if I really want that, I can't create war in any place in myself. Any little speck in me that's trying to create war, I have to transmute and restructure it so that I don't react in a war-like manner to any challenge. Another person was present when my friend was saying he believed in keeping the war going. Actually these people were my brother and my nephew.

This person, my nephew, was very upset afterwards and wanted a debate—or rather he wanted *me* to debate with his father because he was afraid of his father, and he said, *"Well, what if Bush is elected?"*

I said, *"We will continue with our life, with our choices, with our prayers, with our work for truth. And maybe truth is different for each person—maybe for a starving child truth is that they are willing to kill for a piece of bread. What can we do? We will continue to create the person we truly want to be. Whoever is President don't let it stop you from being true to yourself."*

You start right here (points to heart). You look right here. You don't look out there. You don't look at Iraq. You say, *"What part of me is creating Iraq?" "What part of me is creating the prison and the system that is torturing human beings—what part of me killed Sophie Scholl?"* And when you see yourself clearly you don't retreat into self condemnation, you feel remorse and you go to work to transmute yourself. That's where you work—right in the center of your reality.

And you have to look at that in an honest . . . as if it's really true . . . kind of way. And that's where you work to create Peace in yourself. We always have a choice. We always have something we can do. Always. No matter what. And . . . what do we know? Maybe Bush is doing a very good job of waking people up. Because he is epitomizing disregard for human life, disregard for the wretched of the earth, greed in the moment. He's epitomizing those things and he is scaring people right into growing up.

Student: *"So it is like a huge power point—our political reactions to hunger, pain, wounds . . . ?"*

Yes, planetarily speaking we are in a huge power point—constantly being challenged to be true. It makes you look at yourself and say, "What can I do to create the intelligence of God, the beauty of God, right this minute, right this moment—*in the wound?"* And say, "What do I do?" You can remind yourself of "B list!" You go to your B list like it's a life line . . . *"What can I create that will heal wounded love?"*

Student: *"You have to let go of your reactions . . . ?"*

Yes, your reactions are a power point. Your reactions are coming from your deep hidden beliefs and fears. For example, when my brother was very ill we had a conversation—he was in his late 70s and was so upset with me, felt that what I do and believe in is crazy—and he was afraid for my politics. He cared about me, but in his world where belief is the important force, he really feared for my life. And as a young man he had been in the military. He had been on Christmas Island when they dropped the first A-bomb. And the radiation was making him ill. *(He died just recently)* He believed in the military and it killed him. All his life he suffered from radiation poisoning his body, but he still believed in the military. Okay, what do you do with that?

Look at it clearly. It is just a belief. It is not Who He Is. It was like a *fist* in his astral body, in his chakras. A lot of his choices came from that fist. But was that fist him? He believed it was him. That fist was not him. So what do you do? At that moment, I kept saying to myself that this moment was about loving him. And pretty soon I was laughing because I was saying what I meant. The only truth left was that I loved him. There isn't anything to debate when you are in the Light of Love and being flooded by the feeling of Love. *Find what you mean and say it—and become it through the power of the Word.* It didn't change him but it changed me to the point where my energy was very light and graceful. And we both became lighter and shared some laughter. He died shortly after that but when he died we were both at peace.

So, beliefs—I want to read two paragraphs from a Real Magic Class Two handout. This is on beliefs. I'll pass it out.

"You don't have to believe in Magic. Now, what is magic? It's technology—to create a magical result use the technology of magic. Belief is not required in order to practice that technology. There are a lot of books about Shamanism, and anthropologists who study tribal shamanism say this [shamanic ritual] *form of healing works because these people are tribal and they believe in magic. They say magic works only because people believe in it. They equate magic with superstition. But they are wrong; this is not why magic works.*

Magic works because of what the Shamans are doing with energy—they are building, gathering and containing huge amounts of energy and directing that energy toward the result they want. It works because "energy makes things happen". It works. To create magic you have to create energy. Energy is required because it is energy that makes things happen. You can create tremendous amounts of energy by focusing your attention on an intention. This has little to do with what you do or do not believe. So, even if you don't believe any of this, and a lot of people who take this Course start out not believing anything I say, or even believing the opposite, but that does not matter—you can, without having to believe you can, create the energy that will make something happen.

It doesn't matter where you begin. You don't have to begin with belief—you don't have to believe in anything in order to create tremendous amounts of energy. Now—beliefs hold huge amounts of unconscious fixed attention and this unconscious attention is a powerful energy. And this unconscious energy is making the same patterns happen over and over again in your life—energy doing things in your life.

Beliefs seem powerful because they are fixed, glued in place by a fixed attention called "My Identity." That is what your ego is guarding—your identity. Your identity consists of the beliefs you carry about who you are and how you are supposed to be and how the world is supposed to be, how you're supposed to be treated, how you're supposed to treat others—all of your beliefs and conditions. This is your identity. Beliefs tell you what to believe about yourself and about life and these beliefs can sometimes be damaging.

For instance, a belief that you are overweight and that you are fat and that fat is ugly, and you will never be all right until you fix fat and ugly, can lead to anorexia. Any belief that holds yourself hatred is not going to be for your benefit but it will be protected by your ego because your ego protects your identity and that belief is part of your identity.

The existence of beliefs creates an energy loop in your consciousness. This is the energy loop (holds up two fists). Your strongest beliefs are like tight fists of energy in your astral body. Each fist is a belief cluster. No matter what you try to create, your consciousness will keep trying to loop back to those fists because they are so strong. They have been there for so long. You believe those fists are real. You believe. You are a true believer. You believe in your fists.

So . . . you have hit a power point. A few fists come up—and so at that moment you remember that this is a power point and you say. "I choose peace." Nothing happens. The fists don't move. But if you keep saying, and you might keep saying this for weeks or even years. "I choose peace" the fists will begin to change, and eventually dissipate. "I choose peace, I choose peace" you keep saying it, reversing the energy, and eventually all the energy of the fists will dissolve and a new light, a new intention, a new form, will have taken the place of the fists. You will have transmuted a piece of your anger.

Energy loop. When your energy loops back to your ego, and you treat it as a power point, you might change for a moment. This feels good, "Wow, I've really done something. I'm different. I'm free." And then whoop, next thing you know you are back in your ego. "Well that spiritual stuff wasn't real. Well that didn't help a bit" says your ego-mind. You just looped back to your ego.

So what do you do? You might remember that you have to practice. And you remember that and return to your B list. Keep returning to your B list. Just fall in love with your B list. You can always say, at any crisis point, "B List." Don't talk to yourself about it—don't keep reciting all your old stories about life. Practice silence about everything. But make a practice of reading your B list every day, as a meditation. So that the only thing in your mind is B list. These are practical instructions, very practical instructions.

So—what do you tend to do when stressful things happen in your life? If you are taking this Course you will remember that stress is a power point. And remember that at first when you practice power points your attention will loop back to your ego because your ego is protecting your identity and your identity is created by fixed beliefs in who you are and what reality is. When your thought process is still in the old mode of mentally processing thoughts, and you focus on how to fix yourself, and on how to prevent possible damaging outcomes, your attention remains focused in your fixed beliefs because your ego is looping back to the safety of the old beliefs—the fists. The ego protects the fists by looping back to the fists and strengthening them.

The Real Magic practices work to break the loop. And breaking the loop allows the fists to dissipate.

Practice noticing your power points. Break the loop. Power points—if you use them—will break the loop. That's what they are for, they break the loop, and they teach the ego to accept new intentions—an open hand instead of a fist. To create real lasting change you must transmute this existing energy of your unconscious fixed attention. Otherwise it's going to come up with the fists. You will let go of that old unconscious attention for a while but pretty soon, your binge nature, your old nature, will come up and grab the energy, loop back to the old attention, and you'll have a fist in your face, and you'll want that drink, or you'll want that guy that you just broke up with, or you'll believe in your fear; you will renew your belief in your victim . . ."

Student: *"We just love the drama."*

Yes. We can be very addicted to melodrama. That's why practicing and having success is good to notice even if it is a momentary victory. It teaches you to love the drama of creation and let go of the melodrama of ego. Ego melodrama is like, "This is my stage and I'm the star and I just hired you to be a bit player" *(laughter)* or, sometimes, "I just fired you." On the ego's stage, everything is about me, me, me, self importance. You can be living a life of misery and trauma but it is still self-importance. You can recognize what we call melodrama. *(Student raises hand and waves for attention)* Okay, C_____, teach us about melodrama *(student laughter)*.

Student answers: *"I'm not reformed yet!"*

Yes you are. We're all reformed melodrama addicts.

Student continues: *"Melodrama is an amazing way to go completely unconscious and have a hell of a time doing it."*

Yes! *(laughter)*

Same Student: *"It is! It is a drug."*

It is a drug. You get so much attention. You are actually addicted to the attention you get. It's about an unconscious desire for attention that is sometimes insatiable.

Same Student: *"You don't even realize you're in that impetuous place until . . . it's kind of like this whirling dervish—just going through this landscape—and it's like you look back and everything's been leveled. What just happened? And you don't remember."*

That's true. It has its own kind of amnesia. Self-amnesia accompanies this kind of melodrama. *"I didn't say that! I didn't do that! That's not what happened."* And often the person sincerely believes that it never happened—they have forgotten.

Same Student: *"I also think if one, like me, if melodrama was my way of life my ego then says, Okay, another way to get melodrama is that when I go to point B, in the back of my mind I'm thinking, well there's no relief. I didn't get any relief. You know what I mean? So I think, what then?"*

You "don't get no satisfaction?" Yes and how do you practice with that? How do you work with that? Power point? Practice Patience? Give up?

Same Student: *"Yes, it's not like I stop saying it (the B mantra) but I notice that I definitely hook around, 'Why am I not getting immediate absolution from this or just the release of it in some melodramatic way?'*

When I'm told I have to just say, 'Point B' it feel unsatisfactory—like is that it? How disappointing! I can't even name what it is. It just gets too much."

Thank you. Yes, you feel like something has to happen to prove to you that something is happening—you are so stressed, you feel like you are going to break, like something has to give—and so you keep doing your practices and nothing happens and you begin to feel ripped off. You begin to feel unloved again. So you attack the practice or you attack the teacher. This is part of the process of addiction.

But when it is too much, don't stop with "too much"—don't settle for that. Choose to let go of your addiction to melodrama and choose to receive drama. That's a beautifully simple A—B. I mean where do you look when it is all too much? You look within. You *feel* within. Go to your heart. You look at you and feel your way to your heart and you make a choice. *"I want the real drama—my real life."* And what's the real drama? Being true to yourself. Simplicity. The simplicity of creation. It's not complicated. It's very simple—Creation is. We don't have to learn a lot of complex information. The reason we do these classes is because it impacts your ego so much and right now those of you who are new to this are kind of reeling, feeling dopey, and falling asleep. That's because the energy of God is impacting your interpretive mind and you can't keep track of what's happening and what I'm saying and whether it makes sense. That's because your ego is fighting the reality of these practices.

Notice the advanced students—they just sit through class totally attentive. They are trained to stay conscious. And notice me—I could do this for days straight and never flag, never feel tired or stressed. So just notice that often when you're new at this Course you fall asleep in class, or in the meditations. Why? Because your attention isn't trained to focus. And the energy is impacting your ego so you go unconscious. So if you do that, don't worry about it. If you're trained to focus, it doesn't matter how many hours, or days we sit in a class, whatever is going on you'll be relaxed and attentive, you won't get tired. But it is all right to be tired!

Let's take a break.

CHAPTER FIVE

RELATIONSHIPS; BLESSING MEDITATION

This Seminar Tape begins with laughter and a student talking:

Student: "... *when I had my cat that was my most important relationship because it was my relationship with myself*...."

Yes, this is true, your most important relationship is your relationship with yourself. To some degree, every relationship you have is a mirror of your relationship with yourself. But the word relationship, now-a-days in pop culture, has come to mean romantic and sexual, and that is not what relationship is. Everything you have is a relationship. You're in relationship with everything in your life all the time. We are in relationship with this room, you are in a relationship with your car, with your cat, with your dog, with your toaster, with your oven, with your TV. What do you feel when your car breaks down or your TV goes dead? (*student laughter*) Definitely a relationship. It affects you emotionally, it affects how you feel about yourself and your life. It affects how you feel about all your other relationships.

And—what if you get up in the morning and you set up your coffee maker and you're out of coffee.

Student: *"That happened this morning."*

That's probably why I thought of it. I was going to say toaster and I switched to coffee. What happens if toast is your breakfast and you've got your coffee made and your find that your toaster isn't working or you are out of bread? What does this do to your relationship with yourself? We tend to react, to feel vulnerable or threatened or angry. What happens if you buy tickets to a great show and your partner says, "Oh my god, I saw that years ago. I didn't like it."

Look at these moments as opportunities for a new existence. Everything in a relationship is an opportunity. This is where your strongest opportunities are. Opportunities for a new existence. Every challenge, a power point.

C_____ are you going to scream or faint? *(Student is banging on her head with her fists, laughing)* So, yes, these are power points—opportunities to focus in the midst of banging your head. *(laughter)*

So how do you apply these principles and practices to your significant relationships in the moment when that relationship is stressed? I mean those relationships with your partner, with your parents, with your siblings, with your children?

Student: (interrupts) *". . . with your teacher?"* *(laughter)*

Oh yes! These are the most significant others in your life. These are vital moments. If your car or toaster can make you tweak, what can your significant other do? How do you apply these practices?

These are often the times when you feel most out of control. And where you manifest your most determined effort to get the situation under control. When you feel threatened, frightened and out of control, even your most beloved significant other can seem like a *dangerous* other. What do you do? Remember, the ego has one goal and one action—control. Control it, because the goal of the ego is safety. Safety. And human beings are control freaks. This is what we are taught to be. This is the reaction we've mastered—the control freak-out. "I have to be in control or I won't be safe." Sometimes it feels like you will die. Danger all around.

Student: *"When I feel really freaked, one of the B list things that has helped me the most with it all is just choosing to let go. Letting go. The whole thing for me is just letting go because control is my issue."*

Another student: *"One very important thing is letting go of taking it personally and letting go of your fear of being wrong."*

First student: *"Yes, because when I'm in my thing I just feel so righteous and I'm right and I'm angry because no one has responded to my rightness properly. (laughter) And so it—letting go—has been a beautiful, beautiful tool for me. I may just say, "I'm choosing to let go. I'm letting go, I choose to let go." But it is letting go of being right or my fear of being wrong or of control of the situation—all of that."*

Yes, that's it. Being attached to being right. Being attached to taking things personally.

Humor always helps. I used to say, "I'm the girl from planet wrong. It's great being wrong." (*Laughter*) I recommend it. "I'm the girl from planet Wrong and its great being wrong." It's a good one. It really helped me laugh at myself and it helps with significant others. It helps with children. You really feel that you want to be right when you're in it with your children. You just want to say, "Because I say so!" When that is going on in you, stop and consider that you don't have to be right. And realize that *your* program of safety is opposing *their* program of safety. And if this power point is with your children, think what a great opportunity your letting go is for them. That by letting go you might teach them the absurdity of the ego. And to teach them that they don't have to automatically defend when they feel threatened or embarrassed or wrong—that it is all right to be wrong. Tell them that being mistaken or making a mistake doesn't mean they are bad or did something wrong.

Sing the, "It's great being wrong—what a relief it is!" song. (Makes up song and sings it.) *(Laughter)* It works. Teach it to your kids.

Student: *"It's that same thing of how to respond in a power point."*

Yes, in a power point let go of taking it personally. This might be the best thing to teach yourself. That moment when you're fixated, you're attached to taking it personally. "It *has* to be the way I want it." This is the moment to let go of the personal and just witness where you are at.

Student: *"Another thing you have said which is really helpful is, 'What if it was all right?'"*

Yes, what if this was all right, the whole moment. Everything. What if this was all right and you didn't have to make it wrong or right, you don't have to win or lose, what if you didn't have to control everything?

Student: *"It seems like it takes you out of your fix-it belief which is saying, 'It has to be fixed! And to fix it THEY have to change!'—It takes you out of that 'off with someone's head!' mode long enough to go 'OH!'"*

Yes, the first thing you have to let go of is wanting *them* to change so that *you* will be all right. Yes, it takes you out of ego and the compulsion to fix and control all the energy. It is a moment that breaks the ego-loop. In the moment, stop and ask yourself, "What if this was all right?"

Student: *"At that moment you can feel the difference between the attentive mind and the controlling mind".*

Yes, for a moment, you're not interpreting. This is liberating. If it's all right, then your interpretive mind has no place to go. There's nothing to interpret if it's alright. I read an article once where a man had taken his children to McDonalds. And once he was there all his beliefs about McDonalds came up. *"Why does this place even exist? No you can't have two helpings of French fries, French fries are poison."* And all of a sudden it came to him, very simply, "What if this was all right? What if I could just be present and enjoying my children." It changed everything. It stopped him from having to interpret how and why some things are not all right. He became present in that moment and it became real instead of abstract.

Student: *"What about the conflict with McDonalds because with the hamburger they take like 55 square feet of rain forest down. Do you support that? It would be hard for me to be okay with that."*

Well ok, you are feeling very judgmental right now. You are looking at this with your interpretive ego which is assuming that I am okay with the destruction of the rain forest. And you want to make sure I understand how politically incorrect this is and you need to let me know that I am wrong so that you can educate me. And you are also interpreting that saying to mean it is all right that McDonald's is destroying the rain forest. Of course I don't "support" taking out 55 square feet of rain forest!

You are *interpreting*, assuming that I am saying we should avoid or ignore political realities like McDonalds. If you hang on to this stance, it would be hard for you to be okay with saying "what if this was all right." It's bringing up your politically correct or socially correct or spiritually correct beliefs and this throws you into immediate resistance and defense and a place of wanting an either/or solution to this "problem" I have presented . . .

So don't be okay with it! That's all right too. Don't force acceptance on yourself. If you cannot bring yourself to say it, don't say it. But don't get so caught up in politically correct beliefs that you keep something creative and new from happening. Allow yourself to be in the present moment and allow yourself in that moment the space to create something new.

When you are focused on being politically or socially or spiritually correct, you are thinking from your beliefs and those beliefs are creating judgments. This statement—*what if this moment was all right*—says something that transcends all of your beliefs. It says be open for something else, be open for the next moment to happen. You can't hang onto your beliefs and stay attached to your beliefs and still let go of self-important judgment and say, "What if this was all right?" You have to let go of judgment and let go of your self-importance. It takes a person who is very true to themselves not to get caught up in politically or spiritually correct thinking.

I was once extremely political. My political beliefs ruled my life, and being politically correct wasn't popular yet but it was part of my belief system. I have learned so many enlightened things since those days and I have found that there are many places where, "What if this was all right?" would have changed the situation totally by opening up the space. I had one instance that was really powerful because I was in a similar situation of judging and being self-righteous at McDonald's and it came to me to try, because I had just read this article from the man who did this, "What if this was all right?" I just let go of everything and that enabled me to have a loving, intelligent, humorous time being in the moment with my kids at McDonalds.

We went home and sat around. We talked a lot and this night talked about why I didn't like McDonalds. (I had told them the truth about my feeling about McDonalds, just not in a self-important way.) They were relaxed and we discussed why I didn't like McDonalds. And after that, we never went to McDonalds again because of those reasons. The letting go of the judgments and going into "What if this was all right?" created so much space. It created the *creative* space so they could *safely* say, "Well mom, how come you don't approve of McDonalds?" And I could easily and quietly and gently and humorously say, "Because I love trees." I remember saying that, *"Because I love trees!"* And they love trees so they could get right into that.

But if you're there in your judgments and there's something your children want, and you're meeting it with the energy of judgment and your own self-important politically correct stance that you are insisting they agree with, what are they going to do but fight you because they feel attacked and they feel that they are doing something wrong. I can look back and see all the times I was unfair and judgmental with my children and even hurt them just because I wanted them to have the right political or spiritual stance. And they wanted me to listen to who they were. I had a lot of self-condemnation to let go of. By the way, self-condemnation is another form of self-importance.

So, how do you use these teaching in a relationship?

Let go of self-importance. How do you let go of self-importance?

Let go of judgments.

Let go of your fear of being wrong.

Let go of taking things personally.

Let go of attachment.

Let go of trying to influence their beliefs, their sense of the world. Courteously impart your feelings about things but let go of insisting they feel and think the same way that you do. Let them be. This is a rigorous practice.

*   *   *

Okay, what if something happens in a relationship that just drops you totally into your victim? That's what happens in a power point—victim has taken over your consciousness. The place where we tend to feel most victimized is in a personally significant relationship. In a significant relationship your 'take no prisoners' ego stance can do some damage—the best way to transmute this is to work with power points and catch them before you try to level the ground in front of you.

So, say you have a relationship with lack, "My life is full of lack." That's your relationship with life. "My life is full of lack." But suppose you believe, "If I had a partner it would fix my life and I wouldn't suffer such lack anymore." So many people do this. *I lack this, that and the other, but what I really lack is a partner. So, I choose to receive a partner. Once I have my partner, my life will work.* So many people have this challenge of wanting a partner—romantically. This wanting a partner is really powerful work because it teaches you to be constantly letting go. There's so much potential for victim in a choice like this—I won't be all right *until*. . . I am not all right *because* . . . you have to let go of conditions like "until" or "because".

"I choose to have a partner, and I'm going to have one and I choose to receive a partner blessing and it's going to happen and life is good." *(laughter)* Stop right there. Don't go into, "And of course he's going to have blond hair or brown hair, he has to be really cool, and wear flannel shirts, and have a beard." Somebody said that to me recently. Was it you? *(laughter)* Or "Of course she has to look beautiful and have nice legs and be smart but not smarter than me"

Anyhow, as soon as you put a label on it, define it, it becomes you defining it and that definition is a condition and there is no space for creation to create, there is just you saying, *"I have to have this package and the package has to come like this and look like this and be like this . . . and if it isn't like this my lack won't be fixed. If I don't have this partner, I'll still be in lack, I'll be sad and alone and life will suck."* This is what people do and it's crazy. If I don't have this partner, I will be in lack. When the truth is that if you don't have yourself, if you aren't true to yourself, you'll be in lack no matter how great your partner might be.

In our media driven pop culture it is believed that this search for "the one" is the most important focus in your life. To even believe that there is such a thing as "the one" is setting yourself up for wounded love. Who can possible meet your conditions—no one will ever satisfy you, you will be wounded by love over and over again.

So you might need to think in a new way about this word *relationship*. What is the most important relationship you have? Your relationship with yourself. How can you, without trying to interpret what that means, allow the meaning of it to blossom in your life?

What happens if, when there's trouble in a relationship and you start defining the problem, and then defining who's to blame for the problem, and trying to analyze the best way to fix the problem, what happens? What happens is that the relationship takes on the form of your *definitions,* how you define your conflict becomes the shape of your relationship and creates the next moment in your relationship. You have learned the shape of lack and conflict you bring that shape into your relationship.

So—what if, instead, you let go of all your definitions about what relationship should be?

Student: *"Well, that could make it boring! (student laughter) Where's the melodrama in that! (more laughter)"*

Another Student: *"So when you say the important relationship is my relationship with myself do you mean my higher Self? A bigger part of myself?"*

No. *See, you are interpreting!* I mean every part of yourself coming into balance as one integrated whole, true, authentic, Self. What is your relationship with your higher self? What is your relationship with being true to yourself? What is your relationship with your ego-self? How do you be true to yourself and meet the demands of a relationship? A relationship is not something you should be able to make unrealistic demands on—it shouldn't even be possible to make unrealistic demands on another human being yet we all do it. For example, *"You have to change because I'm being true to myself."* Doesn't that sound like an absurd demand. *"You have to change so that I can be true"* really means *"you have to change so that I will feel safe".* That sounds pretty crazy but this is what people do. Why can't you just give them truth and say, *"I am afraid of life without you in it, but I am trying to deal with that in myself."*

This is what your higher self is trying to say. Where does your higher self come in? What is this part of you trying to teach you about relationship?

Student: *"When you are cultivating a relationship with your higher self you have to choose patience. And you have to choose . . . . um . . . . . . patience . . ."* (sympathetic student laughter)

Oh yes.

Student continues: *"You have to choose letting go and you have to choose letting go of self importance and you have to choose all those qualities that are very quiet in a way, very simple and quiet qualities, when allowing something real and aligned with your truth to unfold."*

Yes—patient willingness and patient stillness is the best way to prepare for wisdom from your higher self. And expect an answer, trust that an answer is possible and forthcoming and be patient. Wisdom works in mysterious ways . . .

Student: *"And what if you are having a relationship with your child? Do you use different practices?"*

No—it is the same relationship whether it is with your husband, wife, parent, or your child—or your toaster or your car, or your clothes, or the yellow light that is about to turn red. *All your relationships are contained in your relationship with yourself.*

This means your Self in alignment with your fulfillment, and fulfillment means truth, your authentic being. Some kind of fulfillment of who you are, what are you doing here, why are you on this planet, in this world? It might be that for you your job here is to be in a really great marriage and to embody that kind of peace and goodness that a really great marriage can show to the world. One of my sisters had a great marriage. It was a thing of beauty. And it was very traditional. She was the lady of the house and he made what is called "good money". Maybe it helped that he made money. She thought so—it was everything she wanted. I think they just liked each other, so that long after they were no longer in love, they stayed liking each other—they liked each other even into their old age—and that was their job. I think they were both pretty true to themselves.

Who knows what being true would have been for a desperately unhappy marriage? Or for me? Being a potential spiritual teacher does not guarantee a successful marriage. I was very bad at being married. I was a very good mother but very bad at being married because there was always something else calling me to the point that I couldn't feel connected with my husband. I was very unfair to him. It seemed to me that my consciousness kept growing while he had no desire for consciousness. I held on by believing he should and could change. I had some fierce conditions on him.

But marriage takes two—and I was too unconscious myself to realize how many conditions I was putting on him—I was focused on what I wasn't getting from him. My most essential connection was with nature and with my children and God, and husbands very often don't like a wife who is constantly distracted. We were both projecting such blame at each other. It broke both our hearts.

Being true to your self is a path. It is not something where you fill out the right papers and a license comes in the mail and you know who you are. *It's a path that doesn't unfold unless you choose to walk it.* Your most important relationship is with yourself. This means if you embody authentic integrity then all your relationships will be filled with integrity. If you embody peace your relationships will be filled with peace. If you embody joy, your relationships will be filled with joy. So, being true to yourself is a path of light, it's your life path and you create it as you go.

Sometimes people don't even begin that search for Self until they're 50 or 60 years old. Don't ever think you are too old. It's only young people who worry about, "I'm too old; I can't start this because I'm too old. I can't take this on this late in the game." Isn't that right? Really! Whatever it is, start it now. Start it when you're 65 or even 89! It is never too late to realize that you are a soul on a journey and that what you choose as your means of traveling is very important. (For example, drugs, or alcohol—any kind of addiction—is not a good means of traveling.) Not to worry, just being, if you believe you are too old now you'll be young when you are twenty years older!

Your relationship with yourself—being true to yourself—is the important relationship and it's the way to bring into being all those relationships you think you can't live without. First you live with your truth.

Student: *"Once you have that first relationship though—even an inkling of it, you no longer think you can't live without someone. I can't imagine feeling that way again. My life is so interesting now—and not in a narcissistic way. I mean relationships have come to me since I've tried to focus on self-knowledge—I'm no longer frantically trying to find 'a relationship'—I guess that is what you mean by things just showing up in appropriate ways."*

Right. Things that are true to you start coming to you—they show up in your life in more authentic ways.

Student: *"Could you talk about the pattern of how when we are hurt or angry we want to blame and look for the culprit?"*

All right, yes, that feeling of being sick and hurt, abandoned. You are programmed to believe that if you find the culprit, who to blame, you will feel better.

Well, you won't feel better if you focus on 'blame the culprit.' It doesn't matter *why* you feel sick and hurt. Yes, isn't that shocking? Your feelings aren't what's important here. Forget about why and let go of blame. Let go of it. *Why* is like *because*. Why and because keep you in process. "I feel sick and hurt *because . . .*" Stop right there. Because means you are looking for blame. Stop with 'because'. Let go of 'because'. And let go of 'why' and let go of your endless stories about who done you wrong. Why and because and who to blame keep you in the ego loop and you end the days of your life still playing loop-de-loop with your unconscious ego.

Stop; take a deep breath and say, "I feel sick and hurt." And if you are continuing to blame someone, especially if it is someone you love, you will feel very sick and hurt because your pain is two-fold—you hurt yourself as well as the other person. "I feel sick and in pain—I hurt!" Period. *Don't process your pain! Do NOT process your pain.* Give yourself the one thing you need if you are going to transmute "sick and hurt" into freedom. Give yourself a point A that you can polarize. How do you polarize it? Just say it "My point A is that I feel sick and hurt. Then carry it from there to find the opposite of "sick and hurt." Find what you authentically want to create.

"I feel sick and hurt. This is not what I want." Now you can go to Point B. What intention will polarize point A? What kind of *relationship with yourself* would you like to create? Do you want a relationship with yourself that creates more pain, fear, damage, and anger; more toxic energy in the world? What can you create that would help you be strong and independent and blessed with discernment and compassion? Choose to bring the energy of healing, compassion, understanding, and blessing into your relationship with yourself. This is your magical point B.

Make this a mantra. "I choose to have a relationship with myself that has magic, healing, compassion, understanding, and blessing in it." Are you willing to receive a wisdom self that is a treasure, that is a diamond? You will find that what comes to you in this relationship with yourself is whatever you are willing to receive. What are you willing to receive from life, from yourself? What do you want to be? What matters most to you? That's what is going to show up in your relationships.

For example, "I choose to receive a relationship of health, love, strength, integrity, peace, compassion and blessing with myself, with other people, and with the world." That's a great all time mantra for everything under the sun. Create an all time relationship mantra with yourself, with other people, and with the world and say it every day until it becomes your first waking thought. Because you are in relationship with the world all the time and that's where your true intentions are going to be most deeply felt. This is where your true Authentic Self is going to show up and be counted.

Student: *And we shorten that by saying "I choose to be true to myself."??? . . .*

Yes! Thank you! This is all part of the path of being true to yourself.

And this is very simple, basic, ordinary stuff. I'm not preaching at you because of some high level spiritual idea or ideal that I know and you don't know. I'm talking about what I know. I know alchemy. I know how to transmute energy using only consciousness itself. And I know this because I have suffered for it. What does that mean? It means my basic nature is fierce, high-energy, protective, shy, quiet, loud and opinionated. I have been told that I am fierce because the nature of what I teach requires me to be fiercely focused on truth. But that is no excuse! I have hurt people. All kinds of people. But mostly I have hurt people I love and the remorse I felt when I examined my behavior and choices, when I brought it home, made me practice these practices with dedication once I learned them. And once I began teaching I practiced what I was preaching until I know it in my cells, in my atoms, it's probably in my DNA—or maybe it always *was*.

And I still have to practice. The ego is so strong, so deeply entrenched in our constant daily collective consciousness—and we get tired and stressed and short-tempered—we hurt—and so, we have to be constant gardeners, digging up weeds and planting truth in ourselves, constant warriors fighting for truth in our deepest hearts. We are not perfect. We never know when we will be brought face to face with our deepest fear of truth. We have to fight for truth every moment of our lives. We have to struggle to make every moment of our lives a blessing. Then we will be true and authentic Creators. Then we will be true to ourselves.

Student: *"Could you talk about doing a blessing meditation. I find that in practicing letting go it is really hard to let go of my bad experiences. And trying to think of a good experience is difficult for me. Is this a general rule?"*

Another Student: *"Right! And in doing the meditation looking for Point B, the bad experiences would pile up before I had time to come up with one really good one."*

Another Student: *Same here—I find it's really easy to come up with experiences where I felt victimized. So when I do a blessing meditation, I usually end up treating it like it's a power point—I try to get some good out of it.*

Okay, let's try a meditation—close your eyes and breathe and relax.

Remember an experience where you felt happy or satisfied . . . . Take your time. Happy or satisfied. Just feeling good. It doesn't have to be big . . . I just remembered the first time I had ice cream. Just happy and simple. And hold on to that experience. Just really feel it. Hold on tight to it . . . .

Now—let it go. Whoosh! Just gone! . . . .

Now remember an experience where you were a victim . . . ripped off . . . . betrayed . . . humiliated . . . . All of it, just remember . . . Take your time . . . hold on to it . . . . really feel it . . . all the pain . . .

Now—let it go! Quick! Don't process it—just let go of it—whoosh!

Now keep your eyes closed and remember blessing,—an experience where you felt happy to be in your life. Hold on to the experience of blessing, the experience of happiness . . .

Now let go of everything—all of it—the victim and the blessing—the pain, and the happiness. Let go of all of it. Quick! LET GO!

And think about this moment of letting go as the beginning of a new existence for you. In this choice to be true to yourself your past is also restructured, transmuted. Your victim has less and less power to hold you in your past. Your romanticizing of your bad times has less and less hold on you as you practice letting go without processing your pain. Just let go of your pain—you can—it's allowed—nothing bad will happen if you let go of your wounded self. It is not real! Your Wound is not your Authentic Self.

Allow your real existence to unfold. Your appreciation of your own choices and your own journey gets stronger and stronger in the reality of the life that you are living.

Now try to imagine what beliefs you are carrying about ownership. What is it you believe the world owes you, and what do you believe that you owe to the world?

Alright, think about that. What does the world owe you? This is what we're taught. We're taught to believe that we are owed something in the world. Your mommy and daddy, your teachers, your friends, they all owe you something . . . and you owe them . . . .

Now close your eyes and think about that ownership that we are taught . . .

Now ask yourself this question, "What do you authentically owe yourself?"

Do you owe yourself a life of integrity? Do you owe yourself a life of truth? Do you owe yourself a life of joy? Do you owe yourself a life of doing what is most true to you? What other reason is there for being here?

There is no other reason to be here. And when you practice these truths long enough to actually experience what happens when you focus a thought and change the world, when you actually experience that, then you will know this truth. But you cannot know this truth until you experience it. So all you can do is choose to practice. Choose to keep practicing. Choose to practice your practices; choose to honor your choices. Choose to believe in your choices, to believe in what matters to you, to believe that Freedom is the most important thing in the Universe. And let go of believing that you owe anything or that anyone owes you anything. See yourself doing this—let go very deliberately . . . just let go.

Now open your eyes and look around and stretch.

*   *   *

Your most important focus is this choice to be true to yourself. And as you make new and radical choices and they become real, you discover then that it's the little four-year-old and the seven-year-old, the teen-ager, the young adult, you, all of you is making this choice. This is how real and coherent you become. You transmute all of yourself—and you know it, you know it because your relationship with your past is different and you can feel that difference.

I had so much trauma in my life I didn't believe any of this was possible. For me it was like, *"Okay, God, I'll do your damn dirty work."* You know, I really was awful because I didn't want to do this spiritual work. I didn't believe in it. I knew that it was true but I didn't believe that any one in the human world really wanted to change. But I kept trying . . . I kept trying to change because that is what you do. I kept trying, but I did not believe that I would ever feel any joy, any happiness, any health. And it took . . . and it's still going on; my choices to receive those things—as realities. And I was blessed in that I could not be satisfied with abstracts, with theory, with ideas about reality—it had to be authentic and deep. I did not believe I could have any of these things for many years, a long time, because I could not feel authentic.

I did believe that *you* could. I came to believe that health and joy and truth and compassion and beauty and wealth, and all of that was possible for *you* but I did not believe it was possible for *me* because there was just too much trauma in me. I had an entity and he was like my special friend and I named him the Hateful God. I believed that the only God for me was the Hateful God. And I lived in hell with the Hateful God and all I felt was despair and I did not believe that could change. And it changed. It changed in spite of my beliefs because *I did the practices anyway.* I practiced to the point where I could at least say to myself, "I want those things. I want to be happy." That was a major breakthrough. I want to be happy! I had never been able to say that to myself. I despised people who could be satisfied with 'happiness' when the world was destroying itself. So of course I was unable to say that I wanted happiness—it seemed the ultimate in selfish ignorance!

So I know whereof I speak. When something comes in to your mind that you want, work with it. Work with everything in you, with whatever comes up. Whatever comes into your mind, say, "All right, I *chose* to receive that."

Imagine that you are in a power point and you try looking at the intense feeling and say to yourself, "All right! I *choose* anger. I *choose* unhappiness, I *choose* trauma, I *choose* fat and ugly. I choose to feel self-righteous, I choose to despise humanity" and feel how self-righteous you are feeling and how absurd these choices are. See how absurd you're being and then look at how those thoughts have actually been creating your reality. And then say, *"Okay, I choose self-knowledge!"* Notice the difference in the *feel* of that. Something's going to shift. You'll feel it. Sometimes you'll feel the shift in your chakras, sometimes in your head it'll feel like a Velcro opening and you are seeing the sky. Some of you have experienced that one. Like, *r-iiiiiiiiiii-p*, and you open. Your head opens. Your consciousness opens. Your awareness expands.

Any questions? Anything you want to say?

Student: *"I've definitely felt that way, where I feel like I'm exploding, getting taller. And it feels so happy."*

Yes. You actually feel as if your physical body is different.

The glorious impossible. Go for the glorious impossible, but you don't have to believe any of it. All you have to do is want it—or if you can't believe you even want something, at least be willing to *practice* wanting it.

All right, and this leads right into a question. What does, "Let go of the How and focus on the What mean?"

Let go of the How and focus on the What.

Student: *"It means don't focus on the process."*

Another Student: *"It means let go of outcomes."*

Yes, don't focus on the process, focus on the intention at Point B but let go of anxiety about Point B as the outcome. Don't put conditions on Point B.

Student: *"Does it mean let go of analyzing?"*

Yes, don't try to interpret or look for meaning in everything—that's process. How? Circling around the how, focusing on the how, "How can I do this? Am I doing it right? How can it come into being if I don't figure it out?" And be sure and let go of thinking you have to be right. There is no right way to do it. Don't try to do anything right. If you're having trouble with it, let go of trying. Especially let go of trying to control it. It is a glorious impossible, how can it be controlled?

Let go of trying to do it right because there isn't any right way. There's only your way and you'll find that you make that up in the moment. You'll find the best way for you, the truest way for you to work with your practices. But first you learn them. First you go into the spiritual gym and work out—you learn your practices—then you practice them. Just listen. Don't try to do it any particular way. Just listen every day. Just listen. Listen to point B. Point B is your "What". Listen to the What, let it come to you, let it teach you. Part of your consciousness knows how to receive blessing. Trust in the What. Choose blessing and trust in it—it is a powerful *What*. Why is it powerful? Because against all the odds your ego is carrying and believing in, you are choosing this particular What. No matter what your ego says, you are choosing to receive blessing.

Let go of How and it will come to you as you wander the Fields of Creation; Focus on What and it will come to you on the Streams of Creation. The What is all contained in your relationship with yourself. Don't pollute your own stream. Create a new story about you wandering in quiet meadows, playing in the Fields of Creation, walking alongside a beautiful clear stream, finding the Fountain of Light, Life, Truth, Beauty, and Goodness. This is your What. You are it.

CHAPTER SIX

DOING THE PRACTICES: VICTIM; ATTACHMENT; TAKING THINGS PERSONALLY; PROJECTION

Now I would like to ask you a question. What has been your most difficult experience in practicing the Course and trying to manifest change in yourself—what has been the hardest part of your work with the Course?

Student: *"I think the hardest thing has been remembering, in the midst of some of the hardest times, that the best support is to do the practices and meditations. Now I am finally at a point where when I feel worst, I know that the thing I want to do most is to meditate or to review your writings . . . (pause . . .)."*

Yes! Thank you! That's it—*do the practices!*

Student (continues) *"I have a partially frozen shoulder right now that I have been working on and sometimes I really don't want to do the* [physical therapy] *exercises because it's painful and it takes up time, I spend a half hour every morning, and always about 15 minutes into it I'm so glad that I do the exercise because it starts to feel better and the pain lessens. It's been a real correlation for me, it's like I'm re-teaching my shoulder how to function in a more healthy practical way and that's exactly what the meditations do, they really teach us. And, they give me back my sense of humor, that's for sure. I think of the meditations and practices as like the oil in my world that helps things move smoothly and gives me buoyancy."*

Beautiful—like a luminous lubrication that flows into every cell . . . . beautiful! Thank you! What about you, _____. You've never taken the Course but you've studied with me for many years. What has been your experience with it—you haven't had the structured practices—but we've had meetings and teachings about power points and polarity.

Student: *"Well, I really related to Sally and I would add a little bit more from my personal experience and that is about talking to other people who aren't working with you, doing the age-old trying to get support from friends, which, I have seen more and more, feeds directly into exactly what I am trying to transform."*

You mean they feed into the victim part of it—into your sense of being a victim? Ego feeds ego.

Student: *"Yes. It's been important for me to quit looking to somebody else when I have something that I'm working on that's bothering me, we're all kind of programmed to do that, and now I don't, instead I sit down and meditate or receive some sense of superconscious Guidance rather than calling a friend and I notice that even the little bit that I have talked to other people recently, even when I'm not even asking for support or help, people can still say one sentence that can trigger certain things . . . And I have learned to say, no I'm letting that go and I don't want to focus on that or look at it in that way."*

You have become more aware of when you are being triggered?—And not react in an old way? That's great! Yes, one word can trigger your total ego. You are using it (being triggered) as a power point. How does it feel?

Student: *"Incredibly liberating. It's beautiful."*

Another Student: *"I always feel like I'm coming home."*

Yes, coming home. So beautiful and simple and expanded. And ultimately so effortless. And yet it requires so much commitment. It requires *constant practice* because it, what you experience, is beyond the range of theories that can be debated and talked about. Theories can't help you, ideas can't help you. But we are programmed to believe they can and that creates a tremendous denial. Experiencing your own Self is what helps you—which means you also have to experience your resistant, wounded self and recognize it as *not* truth and be willing to let go of it.

Yes, focusing on the practices is primary. In the beginning this is the hardest thing for students because there is no theory, no philosophy, no proof that says if you do these practices, *something special*, is going to happen—you have to practice radical trust. And so often you have to do the practices in the face of your resistance saying *"nothing's happening, why should I keep doing this? I'm tired. This doesn't make sense. My friends think it sounds pointless, a waste of my time and money. And yeah,*

it's all right for teacher to talk, but I have to live in the @%$#&^$#@ real world"
Right? Talk to me.

Student: *It goes back to power points, constant power points . . . to be in the moment, and for me a big challenge is to watch the news on TV or just things that come up living day to day with all of this "going on" and try to stay conscious and make conscious choices and focus my attention . . . right in the center of the bad feeling . . . I have to remember the bad feeling is not what it is all about . . . the feeling doesn't matter . . . (stops)*

Right! And this requires *constant* practice—until the moment when the past falls away from you and it all becomes simple—just being alive becomes a simple flowing moment. Doing your practices is like learning to play the violin. In the beginning the violin can seem like a dangerous alien, even unattainable or impossible—but at some point you realize that you are playing the violin.

You can move easily through life, watch the news, be more effective in your choices and actions, easily take care of your children, present a project to the board of directors, create the collective endeavor that is dear to your heart, write a great book, all in the midst of your fear—anything you do you can move harmoniously with it because you know who is doing it. You are not constantly projecting that it is about your pain or your fear or who to blame. You know it is about you and that you are capable of creating a work of art life that works for you.

Who is living this life for you and what does this person, this *you*, that is living your life really want? These are the two real questions—one, do you like your life the way it is now, and, two, what do you want? Your whole path is based on these two questions.

And your ego is afraid of these questions because your ego is focused on having to make a judgment, having to decide either/or, this or that? The question is "Is this the situation, the existence, you want to be in?" There is no place where it says "you have to make a *judgment* about this situation." In this situation a simple statement of "No! I do not wish to be where I'm at!" without commentary or editorials is not a judgment—it is a statement that includes a desire for change that leads to knowledge.

Right? You don't have to decide either this or that, for or against. You don't have to decide "how" this can be changed or resolved. It doesn't matter if it's your relationship with your health, with your unreliable car, with your job, with your wife or husband or best friend, or child, or the world situation—it is in your life and you are unhappy, anxious, worried, or angry about it.

And your ego is afraid of it and this makes you angry—you want the bad feeling to go away! So you debate and interpret and ask your friends for advice and none of that really touches the depths of your feeling of angst. And you might never arrive at the truth—the truth being that *it doesn't matter if* you are afraid, it doesn't matter if you are angry. Remember—it is not about your *feelings!* It is about whether or not you want to transmute those feelings, transmute what is making you feel bad. It is about *what relationship do you choose to have with those feelings?*

In this transmutation nothing has to be "solved" because when you change your own inner qualities, the world shifts to resolve the problem in the best way for all concerned. Yes, you are dealing with a very conscious universe—and it is a universe that wants you to prosper. Creation itself will solve your situation through bringing in the energy of appropriate truth. You choose the quality you want to create in yourself and Creation moves to bring it about. Your job here is to trust in Creation—and if you are a normal human being this is the hardest job you will ever have. We are not trained to trust the unknown (and uncontrollable) power of the Universe.

So point A might be, "I don't like myself in relationship with this situation." Point B might be, "I choose trust whatever quality most fits the situation" and then you let go of any obsession with fixing the situation, with manipulating the outcome to make it happen right—and you let go of self-condemnation.

What you are going to learn is that whatever the situation, the thing you don't like is in yourself, it is not about dad or husband, or your wife/girlfriend or the state of the world, it's about yourself and who you *think* you are. This is what all the spiritual cliché's (such as *"You are the answer"*) are talking about. And the fact that this egoic self can be changed is the greatest learning of our age—this is the true meaning of The Great Work. The alchemy of Self-Creation—the human ego can be re-structured through alchemy.

I'm going to tell you a story about myself before I learned the process of Creation and how Creation moves in mysterious ways to help us, no matter how victimized we feel

In the *conscious* creative process, we create a polarity, a map of what we want our attention to focus on, then we create a mantra to help us stay focused. We create a conscious choice and this choice is our agreement with God, with Creation. A conscious choice says you are agreeing to receive—you are saying, "Give me what I am—a diamond."

Well, what happens before we learn these tools that consciously allow us to transmute our victim? The truth is that the Source of all Consciousness is always working with our higher Self in our behalf whether we consciously allow it or not.

My story is that I was pretty much stranded with my children on Lopez Island in a cabin out in the boonies. No electricity, no water, and I did not know how to drive and even had a deep, phobic, fear of driving. My husband was no help because he had become a significant dangerous other in my life. But he did have an old Volkswagen bus. I learned to drive by grinding my teeth and allowing my victim anger to outweigh my terror, by getting in that bus by myself and just doing it—because my fear for my children outweighed my fear of driving. I had to get to the store or we'd run out of food, and what if one of my kids got sick? So I drove.

What I really wanted and was crying for in the wee small hours was someone to be nice to me, someone to love and care about me and my children, someone I could count on, someone to live with who would drive *for* me. What came into being when my outraged, bone deep, fearful, victim chose to drive in spite of my fear? Someone living IN me who could drive.

But I did not feel blessed. Where was the blessing in that? An old Volkswagen and a mean husband who mocked me, whose meanness was energized by my victim, and being miles away from any kind of help—this was the blessing in disguise because it forced me to take action! And it was not until I learned to consciously create a new existence and let go of my deep victim beliefs that I was able to acknowledge that blessing and truly receive it. *Why was that?*

That was my victim self, constantly focused on my "poor" children and my "mean" husband and my fear. Even after I had forced myself to learn to drive and left my husband behind, I still believed that my fear and my victimization had been real! I was still terrified of life and my victim still had a strong voice—only years later could I realize how much opportunity for blessing I had been given—and only then could I say, "Gratitude, thank you". And that blessing began when it occurred to me in a real way, after years of choosing peace and wisdom with him, that my husband was just as afraid, just as unhappy, just as focused on wound as I was—and just as deserving of happiness. The beginning of truth for me—he was not to blame—he was not a dangerous other.

Manifesting will happen, is happening constantly, the world is in process all the time, the world is coming into being around you constantly, and sometimes it's not until much later in the alchemy of your whole life that you realize that you manifested exactly what you needed. When you are most in victim you might receive something that will be the very best step you can take at that point. The Technology of Love isn't about getting everything we *think* we should have, no one came along who would love me unconditionally and do it for me. It is about becoming true to ourselves, it is about doing more and being more than you ever imagined you could be. It is about loving yourself and the world unconditionally.

Student: *"I remember you used to say often; 'Don't attach to the package, what it looks like,' and I think that over time, it's like the perspective shifts and you understand that you're seeing shifts as you go along. It took me awhile to understand that sometimes events are a gift in disguise and to be patient when I thought things weren't happening."*

Yes, it takes a long time to change because we attach. We attach to the past. And we attach to our belief that *something is supposed to happen!* Right? This is a big one—looking for meaning and attaching to the great car or job or loving help you are "supposed" to be receiving—and which is supposed to come from outside yourself. Right! You look at yourself and there you are, calling a mantra and nothing's happening. Or it seems to you as if nothing's happening, nothing's changing. What can you do?

Student: "*One thing you can do is recognize that if it's not happening fast enough maybe you are attached to time and need to cultivate patience.*"

Oh yes, thank you. Almost always, this is about attachment, because we attach to some definition, some idea, to victim, to the package, to how the job is supposed to look, or to how our perfect partner is supposed to look. How our teacher is supposed to look and act. How the hot date is supposed to look. *(student laughter)* And meanwhile the love of your life—or a great opportunity—just walked by and you were blinded by your attachments and didn't see. *(more laughter)*

Student: "*I was thinking that as you were saying that about your story, how important the trust is. And how it becomes so palpable as you go through this* (process) *and see more and more, well, it didn't come out the way I asked for but look what happened instead. Look where that led me.*"

And you realize that something wonderful happened.

Student: "*Yes, so there's this incredible sense of trust that starts becoming bigger and bigger, which is wonderful.*"

Yes, it really is about trust. The first time I got in to drive that horrid VW bus that I hated, it was awful—poor me was so angry and betrayed. I wish that I had known enough to choose trust and get in and just drive without obsessing on my victim and lack. I retained my sense of desolation and loss and of believing someone should be helping me when I could have manifested not only a me who was miraculously driving (thank you!) but a me capable of trust and joy and strength in the moment. This is the difference between conscious manifesting and an older way of manifesting in which God working in mysterious ways forces you to grow—while you kick and scream about your victim! Trust indeed!

Student: "*I've been thinking about attachment, doing the practices, and at the beginning I'd fight with them because I didn't see anything happening. And, where I'm at right now, if I look at my life, it hasn't changed in terms of job, in terms of money, car, partner, I mean nothing has physically changed. But I have changed inside and that is the trust. I don't even have to trust, it's almost as if the word trust now goes beyond itself and I just Know. Nothing's changed on the outside but I have changed inside and I know that. I know the practices are working.*

As an example, I so often don't trust myself when I'm facing others. I have a very controlling boss and the other day my boss asked me to do something that had nothing to do with my work so it didn't matter if I did it or not and I didn't want to do what she was suggesting I do. I had to say No. And she kept asking me. And I had to keep saying No. I was standing at my desk and there was this moment where I said, Okay, be true to yourself. What do you want? So I said No again and she dropped it. It was a powerful experience for me. Then I knew, how can I not be true to myself? That is the most important thing that we have. How can I be untrue anymore? It would be such a sad thing—not because someone's taking advantage of me or anything like that, it's just that I can't allow myself, my spirit, I cannot allow a dishonoring of my True Self anymore. So, nothing in my life has changed—except that."

Except you're free.

Student: *And I'm free.*

So something did happen, you can't say nothing in your life has changed. Sometimes the outer changes radically, in amazing ways. And it is easy to look at that as "something happened" And it is easy to not notice subtle inner change and hold on to "nothing happened". Sometimes the outer circumstances don't change, but the inner life changes so radically that you look in the mirror and expect a different person to be there. It is very important to acknowledge inner changes because they are the most significant kind of change and they indicate the most authentic reality. Don't separate material change from inner change this encourages the separation between ego and Soul, or matter and Spirit.

Student: "*If there is no such thing as too much review, could you talk about the concept of not taking things personally?*"

Oh, yes, that is an important practice . . . very important to let go of taking things personally. We are programmed, as children in school and in our families, to take everything personally—we are taught ownership, that our safety and our strength and our power is in ownership, what we own and that the way to retain ownership is to always be on guard and to take things personally.

When you're a child you own your mother and father, ownership, *mine*. To be told to not take that ownership personally can be threatening. We carry a whole world of beliefs based on ownership and the idea of *not taking things personally* is directly threatening because this belief in ownership—which is a very personal belief—is tied to—attached to—our personal safety and truth.

We must let go of the whole idea of ownership, the whole idea of mine, it's mine. Only then can true, authentic Self evolve, which leads to mutual sharing, mutual being.

This is very difficult to master. I still find myself doing it with my children, wanting to own their choices, make their choices for them—then having my feelings hurt when they are rejecting, or when I perceive them as rejecting closeness with me. This might be the most important practice we do. Let go of taking things personally.

Give me some examples from your own life . . . . talk to me.

Student: "*I have one. Right now I'm taking my sister's behavior toward my parents personally. She's being very aggressive and mean to them. I've been asking what's appropriate for me in this situation and at the same time I realize that it's important that I don't judge or condemn her, that I create the space for a possible different choice just within our relationship. But I have been noticing that I do take it personally. There's always that little red flag where I find that I want to do something about it, I want to talk with her, I want to change it. And then I think, okay, what's going on with that? So that's an example. I just trust that an appropriate format will come forward.*"

Trust, yes. It is all right to talk with her and want to assist all the people involved, but to wait for that appropriate time is true trust. You are asking for discernment rather than judgment—that is what being true to yourself is all about.

Student: "*It's been a good opportunity for me to look at what I'm still holding onto in my relationship with her, but it's hard to take.*"

This is family and family is the bottom line—it is the hardest challenge we ever have to meet. You constantly have to stop and check yourself, where am I, what

MECHANICS' INSTITUTE LIBRARY
57 Post Street
San Francisco, CA 94104
(415) 393-0101

am I doing, am I taking this personally? There is an Arabic saying, *"One's family is like a needle in the heart."* Family is what really gets to you. And not taking things personally extends to everything. When my oldest sister died it really affected me and I went through a lot until I realized I was taking it very personally and staying angry at her instead of grieving and letting go. And so we must let go of even taking the death of our loved ones personally—and we do, we take death very personally because we are so afraid of it.

Let go of the part of loss that has to do with possession—I lost something. You cannot lose the love you shared with them, it is a golden connection that endures forever and as the grief mellows, this truth of love is very comforting and sustains the heart. But truth is not in that deep emotional ownership—mine, mine, mine, and I lost it. The grief might endure for a long time but the loss drifts away when the ownership rights are let go of. They—this person you loved—did not belong to you, they belong to Truth, to Life, to Love, and there was only love, and it endures for both of you always.

Student: *"I'd like to share something interesting I heard. That we judge ourselves by our intention and we judge other's by their impact on us. That's the thing where it's taking it personally. It goes with the assumption that we make . . . , like, you're having an impact on me so I'm assuming that you're intending that to hurt me or that you have bad intentions. And I don't know why I am assuming all these things. That's what I try to think about too."*

Thank you. Yes, this is something we take very personally . . . our assumptions. Our belief that our assumptions must be right and we have to convince everyone involved that we are right. This is a hard one to get yourself out of—it requires total honesty. But what we tend to do—that ego again—is *protect* and *project* our assumptions. What we assume is happening and what someone else assumes we assume is constantly being projected, back and forth. And all we can do is keep on practicing our practices until the day of freedom when we are able to look at ourselves and know we are making an assumption and let go of it.

Student: *"Could you explain projection?"*

Yes. Projection is exactly what it sounds like—a projectile. A projectile that is thrown at someone. This is what a power point is about. Emotion is thrown, projected toward anything that triggers fear—any strong emotional reaction will cause us to project. The fear gives rise to feelings of anger, pain, or panic. Then it is like, *"I have to get rid of this bad feeling, make it go away, so I will throw it off me and since you made me feel threatened, angry, scared, hurt, I will throw it at you."* This can create a very abusive cycle between people.

Student: *I've been just recently really watching that and seeing how disrespectful it is, whether it's us doing it to someone else or someone doing it to us. My daughter had one of her teachers telling her . . . projecting really wild stuff . . . that she was having a really hard time with certain things. My daughter was looking at her wondering, what are you talking about? It was weird. She came home and it really threw her into a spin until she got clear and then later she realized that the teacher had some idea, maybe from her own past at that age and was projecting it, thinking that she was being helpful, compassionate or empathetic . . . She was so far off base and my daughter was thrown off by it and went into a little depression for a few hours to figure it out. And I thought how incredibly disrespectful that is. And yet it's part of our programming to try to empathize and relate and say, oh you must feel this way or that . . . I see and I sympathize . . .*

Yes, and often no matter how well-meaning we think we are, we are actually caught in our assumptions and projecting who we *think* someone else is and how we think *they* feel. It's a violent thing to do, to assume that you know who someone is and how they feel and what they should do about it—(and that would also include your daughter and her (and your) assumptions about and projections toward the teacher). Parents and children do this to each other often. I did—I would assume I knew what my children were thinking and what they needed, what was going on with them, and many times I did, but it was still me projecting my assumptions . . . and many times I was way off, very wrong.

Student: *"Is projection always a bad thing? What if you are projecting love?"*

When you are free of taking things personally and you are full of love or appreciation or caring, you can no longer project because you've lost the projectile muscle—you *express*, you *emanate*, and that is a different energy, that is not a projectile—it's as simple as breathing, you don't breathe because you want to change someone, you are not trying to change anything or enlist someone else in your trip. Live and let live doesn't require projection because there is no urgency for change in it—there is peace in it.

Projection almost always has some violent or intrusive energy in it. *Projectile!* The energy of wanting to make something happen, make someone change or impress someone, create an impact in the world or in a person. Whereas when you are in a state of being true, you simply emanate truth and nothing has to come back to you, nothing is owed to you. No one has to "get it." Projection usually happens when you are trying to prove something, trying to change, convince, enlist, or interfere with others—trying to get something back from them. Projection comes from the ego's fear of being wrong. You are projecting your conditions and expectations. It is a forceful movement of energy.

Student: *"I've been really conscious of projecting lately because I have a friend who tells me that I do it a lot. And since I've been conscious of it I find that the less I've been projecting, that the more people are projecting on me. Like I've had people I barely even know come up and tell me what they think of me. It doesn't bother me much though."*

Hmmmm . . . it doesn't bother you? Is it not a power point? *(student shakes her head)* . . . okay . . . but you *are* noticing that it is intrusive aren't you? Did you invite these people? Did you ask them to assist you by telling you what they think of you? When we become aware of our own projections, we also become aware of other peoples. I don't think more people are projecting at you, you are simply noticing the fact of projection more.

Same Student: *"I don't know that I find it intrusive because if it gives somebody an opportunity to get it off their chest then it doesn't bother me. If it relieves them . . . didn't Jesus say, 'Turn the other cheek?'?"*

Hmmm . . . Well . . . then you might be a saint. *(laughter)* Is it your job to *relieve* them? To be a receptacle for the bad feelings of others? If they vent their spleen—anger and antagonism—on you it is all right because it is relieving them of their toxic waste? I don't think so.

And what Jesus meant when he said "turn the other cheek" was "turn your *conscious* cheek toward them" He was talking about an energy shift. He didn't mean if someone hits you turn your face and let them hit the other side. He was actually saying "Shift your energy; shift your perspective and give them truth."

Projection is always intrusive. They are not creating for themselves, they are giving it all to you, making you responsible for it, for how they are and how they feel and you are doing the same thing to them. So it *should* bother you in some sense. Human beings are not supposed to be toxic waste receptacles for each other. You are not helping them when you let them walk all over you. That is not really what Jesus meant. Turn the cheek of Gracious Wisdom. And kick their ass if they are being intrusive . . . He did not hesitate to take a whip to the money changers in the temple courtyard. You do not have to violate your own integrity for the sake of being "nice" . . .

Same Student: *"I am trying to be compassionate!—aren't we supposed to be compassionate?"*

Compassionate does not mean martyrdom. Compassion does not mean being nice. Compassion does not mean lying down and offering yourself up to be used. There is a lot of common sense involved in true compassion and false compassion without discernment is self-importance in disguise. You are confused about kindness—it doesn't mean allowing trespass. It means kind is simply something you are—not something you do.

Maybe you are afraid of confrontation, afraid of your own violent reactions or your own feelings of anger. I've seen you do this, R___. You are very much afraid of confrontation. And you get very frightened when you think someone doesn't like you or is mad at you. Confrontation is not the same as just simply being true and saying and being what you mean. Grace is the difference.

You might think it's a sign of your compassion to tell yourself that their projections don't bother you—you might think being responsible for their well being is a great and good thing and that it means you are a special person and a healer. I say it is denial and avoidance. You are avoiding being true to yourself. You might have reached a *necessary* point where you are not taking their projections personally, but, *please,* notice that projection is intrusive—practice that much discernment. And give them that much truth. If you are a true healer, then your job is to give them truth. Even if at some level they sense that you have put out a shingle that says "Healer" and you are saying that you are available to them, it is still projection if they use you to vent their fear and frustration. Be sure you are not saying, "Use me!"

Same Student: *"Well, I must be."*

Yes, at some level you are making yourself available to their projections. General rule of consciousness: *Do not be available to usury.* This is a very rigorous practice. As for you, tell them to make an appointment. Say something humorous and true. Ask them to be appropriate, to honor your boundaries. In honoring this you create the high level of energy that happens when you consciously choose to be appropriate.

A boundary is not a condition. By asking them to be more conscious you are not putting conditions on their healing. You are honoring your own intention to be true to yourself and you are not allowing your energy to be used to mop someone else's floor. When you declare to yourself that you are a healer and make a formal appointment with them, that formal appointment creates appropriate boundaries at the appropriate *appointed* hour. This is why therapists don't make their home address and phone available to their clients.

Same Student: *"I have to take that sign off my door."*

Yes, take the sign off the door. Someone like you, R_____ who feels a strong desire to help people, a desire to heal others—if you had a magic wand that could heal the world you would use it. But you are *not* a magic wand so you must develop the quality of discernment. And allow yourself some boundaries. If you allow others to project and say you accept it in the name of peace, or in the name of helping them, you are simply allowing them to use you and it is not helpful to *anyone* if you allow yourself to be used. Discernment means knowing when to say yes and when to say no. You emanate and express the desire to assist others because of who you are, but that doesn't mean you don't also learn to take care of yourself.

Student: "*What about a response? What do you do? You have to respond. If you could completely not take it personally wouldn't it be fascinating to go, 'Wow, how fascinating that you would think that way, but that's not my experience at all.' Or something like that—and then they might see too.*"

You mean they might see the Light? It doesn't matter if they see. That is just as manipulative as projection. Manipulation is a subtle form of projection. That—your approach—is very psychological. Why do you have to respond? You don't. *You don't have to respond.* Who says you have to respond? Did mommy and daddy tell you that good girls always respond. Don't respond. You don't have to explain anything. You are not responsible for them "getting it" or them "seeing" or them "seeing the Light". They will see the Light when they are ready to see. It's not a feather in your cap if your response helps them "see".

Not taking it personally means *no response is required.* If you are truly not taking it personally you do not even notice whether or not they respond to you. If you are looking for a response from them or projecting the response you would like them to make, you have an investment and you are taking them personally. If you do respond, have *no interest* in how they respond to your response—it doesn't have to DO anything.

And this is not what you are suggesting here, you are talking about doing something that will elicit the "right" response from them. If you respond because you believe you have to respond, then you are attached to social programming. If you respond because you are attached to them "seeing" then you are being intrusive and projecting an agenda, an outcome—and you are setting yourself up for disappointed expectations. As long as you are focused on a response from them, you are already projecting judgment.

What if they do not have to see the Light? What if they *never* see the Light and that is all right? This is the way to not take it personally—not being attached to anything.

What we are concerned about is discernment and being appropriate. If you are truly not taking them personally, *then* you have no attachment to how they react to anything you yourself might say or do.

We get attached to wanting to do good in the world, and attached to wanting to be seen as good people, or as smart people, or as effective, or wanting to impress others with how unconditional we are. *(laughter)*. It can become a kind of spiritual status thing. And none of that matters. Sometimes we have to say No, or ask if they want you to teach them and if they say no you let them be—I mean you really, truly, *leave them alone*. Yes, it is true, we want to change the world, we see so much that needs changing in this world and we are teachers—so we first learn to teach ourselves. That's what I do, I teach myself and as I do, I teach you how to teach yourself. That is my job. I focus on my job.

Student: *"One of the ways I've learned how to deal with people projecting at me is through, in my meetings with you, when I'd be projecting at you and in your energy there was no available energy* [responding] *to me, no place for that to exist, so I had to learn what that felt like—You weren't responding to my hurt feelings or to my self-importance. And at the same time I realized that by you not engaging in that, it allowed me to make different choices and that it wasn't judgmental of me. And you're right, a lot about projection is need: 'You have to take care of me, you have to love me.'"*

Yes—"You have to make me all right. You have to fix me. You're not supposed to scare me, or hurt me. You are supposed to love me *in a way that I can recognize and that makes me feel better.*" Wow!

Student: *"Yeah. There are friends that I have who have a lot of victim energy and they'll be talking to me and the only response in me is silence and it's an interesting dynamic to become comfortable with that. When you're not available to that energy and you're not condemning them, you just don't know what to say, you don't know how to respond so you don't respond—and it shifts in and of itself."*

That's great. Yes, you don't have to do or say anything to fix it, it will shift on its own. Let go of wanting to psychologically fix it. The more true to yourself you are, the more the energy around you shifts appropriately in appropriate ways. And it becomes easy the more it is practiced. Just not being present—don't show up to engage in projection. Be available to the truth in the moment. Staying still creates tremendous energy.

Student: *I've been going through another challenge with this health thing. I've enjoyed hearing what others say because it's just reminding me that I realize I have what I need to heal and to begin shifting. But underneath all that it's not shifting because I'm not comfortable with being sick. And it's more than just "what do I want to create?" It goes further than that, it's like taking a big leap into my true life which is being true to myself and this is why this is a throat thing, and a back thing . . .*

Hmmm . . . what could be more than knowing what you want to create? What could be bigger than your . . . .

Same Student. (Interrupts) *Well it is . . . ! Well it's huge you know . . . that I'll get meningitis again. It's scaring me. And you keep talking about it, and it just makes me mad."*

I keep talking about it—you mean I'm talking about you getting meningitis? And it makes you mad—it's my fault—I'm scaring you?

Same Student: *"You've brought it up a couple of times and it's really pushing my buttons."*

Then it is a power point. If you work with it as a power point, you could think in a different way about the fear—maybe the fear has to do with your relationship with meningitis—and so the fear isn't my fault—it isn't anybody's fault. Why not trust that the fear can be transformed and you can create a new relationship with meningitis? Why didn't you tell me that I was talking too much about meningitis? Why didn't you ask *yourself* if I was doing it consciously? Why didn't you try to shift out of your victim???

Same Student: *"Because you're my teacher."*

Because I'm the teacher, you mustn't try to shift out of your victim? You have to stay in victim so as not to bother the teacher? Well then, if you really believe that, I'm not a very good teacher am I?

Well . . . if I'm the teacher, I'm willing to be the teacher. So as the teacher I say you can say anything to me because it's my job to not take you personally and also to assist you. You can say anything . . . But as the teacher, I am *not willing* to allow you to stay in victim mode . . . You can trust that. As the teacher, I promise I will not allow you to stay in victim . . .

So, first of all, I didn't do anything to you. You pushed your own buttons. Instead of taking your fear, and my blame, personally, drop that now, let it go, and say to yourself, *"All right, there's self-knowledge here for me and I want to know what it is. Why does it make me so angry when the teacher says meningitis? What am I afraid of? I want to find the knowledge in that. I want to transmute that fear."*

Of course, I don't remember saying it at all, you know—you have to tell me because I can't remember everything I say. *(laughter from students)* Perhaps the truth of it is closer to: *"Why do I believe teacher keeps talking about meningitis? What old belief and fear is being triggered in me by that word?"* Did you think I was judging you?

Same Student: *"What I was doing with it was taking it personally and trying to fix it, just like all of us do. You know what I mean . . . something's wrong so it must be me that's wrong, it's something that I'm doing wrong, so I'm taking it personally, and then getting sick and my back and neck going out at the same time . . . I don't know . . . all that . . . It's just all that . . . that whole thing . . . fear and trying to fix it all . . . all at the same time . . . but I know that . . . or I think I should know that . . . that I have the gift of this Course . . . and . . . "* (This was being said with accelerated fear, faster and faster, almost hysteria, she was feeling overwhelmed—she was in a power point.)

Stop! _____ stop! Look at me! Look at me, please . . . .

Same Student: *"I can't! I have to think about what I'm saying."*

Look at me! . . . Be still. See? You don't have to talk. Just be still . . . . what do you want?

Same Student: (gives up and sighs deeply) *"I just want to feel better."*

Good!—*you want to feel better. Do you want to feel at peace and healthy and strong and happy?* This is a power point. Are you willing to release your past? Are you willing to release meningitis? Are you willing to release fear and blame? Are you willing to receive everything that is truly yours, your beauty, your strength, your gift of wisdom? Are you willing to receive that? Are you willing to make the whole class cry? *(student laughter—tearful and commiserating)*

Same Student: (tearful) *"It's so hard to hang on and be in control."*

(laughter—commiserating, from other students) Oh yes, it is very hard to hang on and stay in control. This is wonderful. What a wonderful teaching you've made available for the class.

Same Student: *"This was really profound. I suddenly got that the hardest thing is to hang on and be in control. I had this wave of dizziness come over me again. The other night I had it and it was profound. I thought it must be my ear and I thought why don't I have an earache? I was so dizzy I could hardly stand up for about 3 hours. (laughs) it was weird. And I just had a wave of it just now . . . my whole world . . . I shifted . . ."*

Yes. This is big, this shift, and your body reacts. Yet, at the same time, is it big? Isn't it simply the divine order of healing, transmuting, bringing balance and the simplicity of just being true. So simple.

Same Student: *It's me and my proper sense of 'take care of the teacher'.*

Yes, there is that, that arrogance of the ego. You know, teacher is fine, let go of that. You were talking out of your old body, the self-pity body, because you have a big change coming up, coming through you and it's magnetizing your old body. So let's work on releasing your old body. This is a natural, organic process in the divine order of transformation.

At any moment when we are on the verge of a major change, our old ego body can take over and that means our old world agendas take over and we are projected into the past. This is projection—another form of projection, one you inflict on yourself. Inflicting all the old assumptions and ideas and beliefs about who you are and what is happening.

So don't let anything, especially your old ego self, your old way of thinking, prevent you from being available to the truth that you are seeking.

So—D_____, don't take your fear of illness personally. And this is hard because that "M" word was a really frightening experience for you. You need to laugh at it, call it the "M" word and know you are not going to do it again, you don't have to do it again but you are going to receive the freedom that is possible from having had that experience—you are going to receive the self-knowledge. You are receiving it now.

These are important moments when there is a big piece of your old self trying to drive you into your past—and this is because there is a large change coming up, a large change is happening in your life. This is when your consciousness senses that change and tries to run into the past, run into an old story—and that is when the practices teach you to say, *"What am I doing? What's going on? It feels bad, but is it bad? What is it I want, not what I think I want, or think I'm supposed to want, or feel afraid of or angry about—but what is it I really want?"*

And at this point you need to recognize that you are in a power point and you are not being available to truth—but that you want to be available—you want to live in trust, to trust that truth is in you and truth is what you want and you are going to do whatever it takes to avail yourself of truth. Just say, "I'm available, give me what I am." And who you are will show up, it will come. It will come because of your willingness.

But the attempt to control it will only intensify the conflict, intensify the pain and fear. So it really does come back to the two questions—Do you like yourself and your life the way it is now? And, what do you want? Then you practice willingness. And think about this: "Why did you become a nurse when you really dislike sick people and you personally resent illness?" What are you trying to transmute in yourself?

A Different Student: *"I was just thinking about this past month when I called you and I was having a hard time. It felt like I was just too close to the mirror, I couldn't see it. When I called you I didn't really know what I was doing, I knew I wanted to talk to you—and you just laid it out for me, which was great. But at that point it was really hard to hear, it was subtle but big—or it seemed big, and too close to my face.*

Thank you. That's a good analogy—too close to the mirror. And so you were aware that you weren't available to truth and you phoned me and asked for some truth, asking me to lay it out for you?

Student: *"Yeah. It was kind of an ass-kicker." (laughter from students)*

Another Student: *"Sometimes when I email you and am caught up in ego mode—and of course people, friends are saying things that are feeding that ego perspective . . . It would increase my thinking of whatever was going on. Then I'd email you and you'll send me this kick-butt answer and I usually just burst into tears and all of a sudden it's like it comes to a peak—and your wisdom and your clarity and your thousand exclamation points!—gives me a look at it and then I think, Oh my God—and all those little things that friends have been saying that fed my victim perspective dissolve—what you said just burst the whole bubble and burst the whole thing.*

And you can't hold on to it anymore.

Student: *"No. Pop, it disappears!"*

Yes! And this is how you learn to do it yourself. Just say, "Pop!" *(laughter)*

CHAPTER SEVEN

BELIEFS; THOUGHTS AND THE BRAIN; WATER; INTENTION; THE LAW OF DEFINITION; BLESSING POT; ALTARS; DRAWING THE ENERGY MAP

S tudent: *"How can we really know we are being just and fair if we aren't able to trust our judgments? How can we learn to let go of being judgmental?"*

There are many levels of judgment in the world and the best thing we can do is cultivate the ability to discern what is appropriate and accurate in each particular situation. Discernment is actually good judgment—discernment refers to wise and accurate judgment—seeing "what is" and making wise choices about it. Which is, of course, mindfulness.

Since most thoughts and judgments are colored by emotion it is difficult, when there is a degree of emotion involved, to know whether judgment is fair. Judgment is often guided by the beliefs and experiences that make up our world view. In order to live without being guided by your highly colored emotional judgments you must practice letting go of taking things personally.

One of the best ways to let go of thinking in a judgmental way is to work with your thoughts and emotions consciously by picking a quality for the day and using that quality as a mantra to guide your thoughts throughout the day. As you pick a word (a Point B) to live by for each day, you are setting up an energy that will bring that word and the experiences attracted by that word, into being.

(Responds to student) Yes?? Are you doing that? Yes, the word for the day. That's really a powerful and effective practice, to pick a quality, a word for the day. And you can carry that further and pick a first waking thought that has to do with letting go of judgments and cultivating discernment. Imagine this—what thought would you like to wake up to? Your first waking thought—just as you are beginning to

come awake. Just as day is dawning, what thought do you want to have drifting into your conscious mind?

Student: *"Is this even possible? Is it possible to work with our thoughts in our sleep? If, as we keep hearing about now-a-days, if it is our thoughts that create reality, what about the thoughts we dream about and the thoughts in our sleep—does the mind keep to some form of thinking in our sleep?"*

The brain maintains some form of activity all the time, even when we sleep. And yes, our thoughts are creating energy all the time. Thoughts follow our attention and attention creates energy. And, as we know, energy combined with thought brings *things*—form—into being. These energies make up what we call the aura, or astral body. The astral body is the energy of thought forms—our personal astral body is created by the thoughts and beliefs that are attached to us, are part of our consciousness. The best way to work with our subconscious thoughts in our sleep is to pick a first waking thought every night. This helps counter the highly active emotions that color our subconscious astral body.

How? Before you go to sleep, think about your thoughts and what your thoughts are doing to the atmosphere, the room you sleep in, the people you sleep with, the house you live in. Remind yourself that as you sleep the subconscious thoughts you project are taking on a life of some sort. So before you go to sleep decide and choose—what do you want your first waking thought to be? This is a practice that will, with *practice*, guide your thoughts all night long.

And if you combine the daily word with the first waking thought, these two practices, combined with power points are the most powerful attention you can give to your transmutation. But of course you have to do the practices and not just read about them.

You know by now that you have to do all your practices, at some point you're going to realize or you already have realized, that you have to do the practices consistently and constantly if you are going to transmute anything. Otherwise you are just a talking head, mouthing words, running words through and out your brain. Practice creates energy and you know the rule about energy—what is the Law of Energy?

Students: (simultaneous chorus): *"Energy makes things happen."* (laughter)

Yes—energy makes things happen. If you want to consciously create energy, *do the practices*. Practice choosing things you need that come up as you go through the day and you will find that making choices and having them manifest will become a habitual way of thought. When you have mastered the practices, changes will happen without your conscious attention because *your attention is influenced by a new creative thought process in your brain.* You will find that you have restructured your brain and your thoughts are following a new pattern.

Don't take your practices for granted. Set aside time for a formal and devotional relationship with your practices. Make an altar. And here I want to again mention blessing pots. Many of you know what that is. It's a good thing to have a blessing pot on your altar.

Student: *"Tell us about blessing pot."*

A blessing pot is . . . you want to think of it as a container, an alchemical vessel, that holds the mantra energy that you have gathered—the energy of your conscious choices. The concept came to my attention when I was in Africa. We were visiting a medicine woman, a Mamissi, and watching her work. She was creating what she called a *conjure pot.* She would ask the client their intention, ask them their wish, what they wanted. And then she would put in the pot things that represented them and their wish—feathers, and beads (she told me the color in the beads was the important thing—to match intention with color and emotion with color). This was a form of color therapy. And she would add some of their hair, drops of their blood and drops of her own blood were included—you know, this *was* West Africa, it's a very organic religion. When she completed the filling of the pot to her magical satisfaction, she would then seal it and give it to the person along with a daily ritual to do.

One particular woman Mamissi was working with was suffering through a painful divorce. So Mamisi said, "Well, where do you want to go?" Her son was interpreting for me and that's how he interpreted it: *well, where do you want to go?* Meaning: What do you want? What do you want your life to be now after the divorce? Where do you want your energy to go? She was putting rocks and beads and things into the conjure pot and she would say this represents such-and-such—like, your children, she had three very symmetrical pure white pebbles that she used to represent the woman's children. Mamissi blessed the pebbles and put them in the pot and made that connection with the woman's children so the children were blessed. And everything that went into the pot was blessed by Mamissi before it went into the pot. She covered it up, sealed the pot, gave it to the woman and the woman was supposed to—many times a day—hold the pot, her conjure pot, in her hands and say some ritual words and know that her new life was safe in the pot and the Spirits were taking care of it and bringing it to her. It was great. It was beautiful.

So as I watched her work I thought conjure pot was a beautiful, creative concept, a brilliant ritual. And decided I was going to use this in my teaching and call it a blessing pot.

So place a blessing pot on your altar—it can be any kind of container, a big pot or a little pot—the only requirement is that it be beautiful to you. It needs a cover—this is very symbolic—if it doesn't have a cover find a nice cloth to use for a cover. When you do your ceremony of reciting your mantras, write your mantras on little slips of paper, put them in your blessing pot and cover the pot. I recommend doing this every so often. Some people create a blessing ceremony to do once a week. And every day hold your blessing pot or focus on it and recite your mantras. This is your own blessing ceremony so make it as beautiful as you can.

This is a very powerful image to use in your power points. In a power point you can remember your blessing pot and visualize it. As you visualize this beautiful vessel *(imagine it as the ritual vessel used in alchemical ceremonies—that which is to be transmuted is placed in the vessel and heat—attention/energy—is applied)*, imagine that everything you want to create in that vital moment is covered and taken care of. You can say to yourself in a power point, "My point B is in my blessing pot and (God or Spirit or Creation) is watching over it—or, my B list is safe in the Cauldron of the Mother." The Cauldron of the Mother is a Celtic concept and it is a beautiful concept and pretty much in the same spirit and origin as the blessing pot. Put your wishes in the Cauldron of the Mother and She will watch over them and bring them to you.

Student: *"Sort of like a Superconscious crock pot."*

Crock pot, yes! Right! You can say, "My new existence is safe in my Superconscious crock pot." Have fun with this.

This is a really effective tool. And it's a very good practice for couples to create a blessing pot for the life they choose to create. "What can we create for our beautiful new existence?" Create the blessing pot and put it in a special place of honor in your home. And in mutual power points you can look at each other and say, "Blessing Pot" It's totally effective. And it encourages you to create an altar because your blessing pot is beautiful and exciting, you will love to look at it. It is inspiring to create an altar around things that represent blessing and beautiful abundance.

Altars are very effective tools for creating and containing the energy of your new existence. Think of your altar as the creation of a holy space around you. A place you can walk into, in the midst of time/space life and be still, peaceful and bright. A space that represents the holiness of, and the reality of, your new existence.

Your altar is a space of intimacy, an intimacy that you can sit down with and add to the energy every day. You don't even have to do anything but sit there and breathe Light and feel a sense of being true to yourself. That's all you have to do. Say some magic words, "I choose peace and patience." Or some similar all inclusive mantra like, "I choose to be true to myself."

One of the helpful things about a blessing pot or a collage or an altar is that it gives you a visual to match the verbal and mental mantra work. This helps you focus as challenges come up on your Path through the Course. Each class in the Course creates a lot of energy and you'll find yourself noticing things in new ways or having a lot of hidden "stuff" come up—feelings of anger, or anxiety—and you want to say to yourself: *"alright, this is energy doing things, I'm changing, I'm in the oven, my life is in the blessing pot and things are changing."*

You are conjuring a lot of energy and you want to use all the available energy that you are conjuring. And the energy of power points helps you keep your eye on what you want and helps build more and more energy toward the creation of Point B. Using power points is like putting money in the bank. You want to do it very deliberately. Practice humor, practice peace, patience. Remember that the real polarity is *you; you are the polarity that is being transformed.*

Make a visual of that. A visual map. Remember, when you polarize and write down your point A and point B, you create a visual map of what you want your consciousness to do. You can also create an image that fits point A and an image that fits point B and put it on your altar. Or, for instance, make a collage around those polarized points and put it on your wall. These visuals are good focusing tools. Use anything that helps. There is a battle going on between your ego and your Spirit. So don't project—don't project blame, don't project anxiety—don't project anything. Practice noticing when you are projecting and choose a word for the moment to replace the projection. Work with every thought that comes into your mind. Yes? . . . .

Student: *"How do you tell when you are projecting? I am reading The Hidden Messages in Water and it is helping me to understand the concept of projection. I was thinking of the Law of Definition—that we are constantly projecting real definitions of real qualities that are being picked up as vibrations by the rest of the world—and this is creating the world—and always has been. It is a wakeup call to finally realize the power of projection—how real it is and what we are creating when we project our emotions."*

Yes, thank you—*The Hidden Messages in Water*—I planned to bring that book today and I forgot. It is in the "Bleep" movie and is a beautiful portrayal of actual thought forms—actual portraits of our emotions. This is what I mean by astral shorthand. Thought forms of emotion that vibrate in the world. Nothing is hidden in the world of astral form. When I was a child I used to believe that snowflakes were like shorthand messages from God sending us little scraps of beauty. This is exactly what a snowflake is—hidden messages from God.

Water used in such a conscious way can be a healing miracle. When I used to work as a hands-on energy healer, I kept receiving from Superconscious or Divine Guidance the instruction to "*burn the water*" and then to have the client drink the water. So I'd have people bring a gallon of water and I would burn the water. I didn't even know what that meant but I would just put my hands on the jar of water and I would get this wave of intense energy pouring through me, it would feel icy cold in my spine and in my hands. But Guidance told me it felt cold physically because the energy was of such high intensity, such high frequency, that it would burn if I felt the full effect.

It was—as are all true things—absolutely simple. I would just hold my hands on the water container and I'd feel strange intensities in my spine, and in my arms and hands and the back of my head. Then I would give the water to the client to drink. It felt very blessed. Sometimes afterward my eyes would feel burning and I would see rapidly shifting images similar to those in the *Messages* book. Sometimes my arms would be shaking so much I couldn't lift things and it would take a while for the sensation to go away and my eyes, hands, and arms, my body, to feel normal. I don't really know how it affected the people receiving the water. I was to instruct them to imagine the water pouring into their chakras and cleansing and healing their energy body. Later on I ran into a healer from the East Coast who had learned to do the same kind of water healing. Water is an amazing substance it its ability to mirror energy, take on form—it is a living mirror, the Water of Life.

I also learned around this time, that the Australian aborigines, the healers, referred to this same icy sensation and the consequent weakness as "Boiling Energy" and described it much as I described it. They would access it by dancing for hours. I would access it by intense stillness—a meditative state.

So the *Bleep* movie and this *Hidden Messages* book reminded me of that period in my life and I thought just imagine if we did that with our water all the time—we could transmute anything in the world. Practice doing energy studies with water. Hold it while you meditate. You might be able to see, as you practice meditating, you can "see" a sensation of light changing in the water. It's beautiful. When I was doing this practice, the "burned" water would fill with Light. I became aware that there was a molecular change in the water. There would be radiant awareness—it would appear in the water. Superconscious radiant water. Radical Light.

So practice doing that. Our hands are amazing. Practice doing the self healing, like—hold your hands like this (like a bowl), close your eyes and feel the energy building, building, building and building, sometimes your fingers will ache, or tingle, or feel heavy. Then lift your hands, lift that bowl, and just give yourself a rub down with the energy you have gathered in the bowl of your hands. It works. It really works. Use it to massage children or pets—loved ones—they really respond in a strong and happy way.

Student: *"I would be afraid I would pick up something negative and pass it on."*

Remember the power of Intention and keep your attention focused on Light and there will be Light! Sometimes it helps if you light a candle and keep your gaze on the candle. The ego is afraid of Faith and Trust. Don't argue with your ego—emulate your Spirit and practice giving yourself the freedom to be true. Ask for Guidance. What if you could not make a mistake? *What if it was impossible for a mistake to enter into your true intention to assist a loved one?* Love yourself that much. You are worthy. You are Radical Light—Radiant Awareness. Live the kind of life you want to live and stay in touch with your true intentions—those you know about and those you don't know about—and practice radical trust. If you are Radical Light can toxins hold out against you?

Student: *"Earlier when you were asking about doing the word of the day I started thinking that is a wonderful practice . . . It's like in the [Bleep] movie where he creates his whole day. One man, that was great, what he was saying . . . of creating his day. Do it with that word, or with your first waking thought, meditation, a word when you wake up. It creates your whole day."*

Student: *"One day when I woke up I thought, "I want to be spoiled rotten today". (laughter) I never would have thought of that, and it was the weirdest thing, it was a fabulous day. I was pleasantly surprised! This is great homework."*

Oh, yes. Nice. That's very nice. Yes—*"let me be surprised, but let me know it's you"*—that wonderful statement is from the *Bleep* movie. I hope all of you get to see this movie. *"What the Bleep Do We Know?"* Have you seen it? I thought you were nodding. Yes . . . ?

Student: (Nods yes) *"I've seen it three times."*

You know, I feel very happy sometimes when I think back to 1978 when I started formally teaching. When I think back, I realize that we *have* changed the world. The world of today is very different from the world of 1978. And in 1968, when I became obsessed with changing the world, I could never have imagined the world of today. Everything has changed in very subtle ways.

*   *   *

And now let's do a transmuting meditation. So, now close your eyes. Let's do a little focusing practice.

Begin to focus your attention on your right hand. (Pause) Imagine the energy building in your hand as you focus your attention. This is energy doing things. (Pause) Now focus your attention on your left hand. Energy moves and follows your attention. Hold that energy in your left hand. (Pause)—Now focus your attention at the top of your head. (Pause)—Now imagine a ball of Radiant Light appearing at the top of your head. (Pause) Radiant light. (Pause) Now imagine that ball of light focused on your forehead, . . . Radiant Light. (Pause)—Now imagine, shift your attention, imagine that you can shift that ball of light, move it, shift it to your throat, a ball of Radiant Light in your throat. (Pause)—And now again, shift that ball of light—move it into your heart. (Pause)—And now shift that ball of light to your solar plexus. (Pause)—Now to the base of your spine. (Pause)—Now shift that ball of light to your feet and hold it there. Imagine that ball of Radiant Light becoming brighter and brighter as it receives the highest light from the earth—and that light from the earth merges with the highest light within that ball of Radiant Light.—Now allow that Ball of Radiant Light to rise

And now hold your hands together, palm upward, at about the level of your heart chakra. And imagine that ball of Radiant Light settling into your hands—the most Radiant Light you can imagine in the palm of your hands—expanding, merging, getting brighter and brighter as you hold this Radiance becoming One Radiant Light—Your hands are Radiant Light . . . . (Pause)

Now take your hands of Radiant Light and slowly lay them on your heart, cross your hands on your heart. Slowly . . . . slowly . . . . gently . . .

Now lift your hands to your forehead, Radiant Hands,—slowly—move to the top of your head, brushing back from your forehead, over your head, brush yourself with Radiant Light,—slowly—down the back of your neck, across your shoulders,—Radiant hands. Slowly—rush them over your face, hold them over your eyes, lightly palm your eyes and feel refreshed,—you are feeling so refreshed. Radiant Light is so refreshing . . . so pure . . . . Just sit with that for a bit . . . . Now take a very deep breath—and another deep breath.—

Choose to be awake and alert. Shake out your hands. Open your eyes and stretch. A really good stretch and stand up and shake out your whole body . . .

Student: *"Beautiful. And as we were meditating I remembered, I remembered something . . .—And now I lost it . . ."* (long pause)

Did you want to ask a question?

Student Continues: *"Oh! I do . . . yes! I was thinking about the Bleep movie. I thought that it was pretty interesting when they showed the neural network and the exchanges and how through association we build a network of these nerves and pathways and with outside stimulation this network starts firing and this is what a conditioned response is, energy flowing through those networks, firing—and they respond. Does our belief system create these paths? And through this Real Magic process of transmutation can we reroute or create new paths? I think I was seeing that in this meditation."*

Yes, yes, this is what transmutation is. In the process of transmutation, you actually create a new neural network—this is what I mean when I say you create *a new thought process*—new pathways in your brain. Yes! This work actually creates new pathways—new synapses and new responses. And not only that, the old pathways *dissipate* because they are no longer being "fired". This is what we are doing as we practice this Course. Restructuring our brains. Transmuting the old, building the new. This is why we use the Polarity Principle.

Student: *"I thought that was fascinating. This is fascinating!"*

Yes! That the brain can be changed is wonderfully fascinating. This is something we are learning about the brain. It's constantly changing and it can be changed consciously and it can be changed by working with our thoughts, by focusing the direction of our thoughts and by repetition of a thought. Mantras—new intentions—actually restructure the brain.

Student: *". . . and you get new neurons?"*

Right! Yes! You get new neurons! The brain can heal itself. There are great new things now being learned now about the brain. It was once believed the brain couldn't heal after a head injury or stroke, that the brain was static. It's wonderfully freeing when you realize that the brain is never static—it has something the brain scientists call neuroplasticity—the physical brain—chemical and electric—is more alive and more creative than we have believed was possible. It might be that the next discovery will be that the mind keeps the brain whole. And that working with our minds we can restructure our brains and create anything. Intentional Meditation will be all we need.

This is why I emphasize doing the practices all the time—power points, meditation, focusing attention and intention, mantras, etc. Your practices attract the energy of self-revelation. And it is those deep revelations that actually imprint the new brain. You want to keep an experimental attitude (rather than an anxious expectation) toward doing spiritual practices—and the practices will allow you to experience a—an experiential shift—the experience of revelation.

Student: *"Makes you believe in this work. Could you talk some more about how beliefs tie in with transmuting the brain? Do our fixed beliefs make it hard for the brain to change?"*

Oh absolutely. Yes, beliefs do make it hard to change—and this is why someone with a flexible attitude toward belief, who can handle contradictions and let go of analyzing every moment, who doesn't need to exist within a rigid set of ideas and definitions and who can release self-control and resistance to change, will tend to more easily manifest change and create a new existence than someone who is locked into resistance—and by "locked into" I mean you believe in your own resistance—you don't believe that safety is possible because you believe that your safety lies within your resistance—therefore, your resistance is *real*.

Student: *"Well isn't it real?"*

No. You *believe* it is real but it is an illusion. Resistance is a by-product of what you believe to be true about reality. Anything that goes counter to your deep reality—your beliefs about what is real—is resisted. Resistance comes from the subtle opposition in the ego toward new thought, this opposition is countered by the Light of revelation and self-knowledge that comes through in meditation. Self-knowledge is required to free yourself from resistance.

Student: *"I wanted to say something after that transmuting meditation we just did. Then you just said the "light of revelation" and in the meditation—in fact in all our meditations—you are constantly referring to Light with a capital L. Isn't Light just as much an illusion as our resistance is? You say Light is real but is it real? You say the ego resists Light. Well, what is Light? And why does the ego resist it?"*

The word "Light" has come from teachers and visionaries down through the ages speaking about their own experience. And I can tell you from my own experience that there is just no other word for it—Light *is*—and it is *Light!* It is impossible to describe—the only word for the visionary experience is "Light".

In the Alchemy of Consciousness, Light is the means or *vehicle* through which subtle forms of information can be exchanged. It makes subtle communication possible through a kind of universal shorthand or code that is stored in filaments of Light and transmitted to all parts of the Universe. These filaments look like beads of radiance strung on a string of luminous Light. It is the same principle as DNA—a means by which information can be stored and transmitted, carried as *filaments of light* or information carried as strings of interacting chemicals, enzymes, proteins and such, both principles exist as a means of subtle communication—beyond the dense physical structure. DNA is manifest Light—the first manifest form—genetic coding. Light is manifest Consciousness—the means by which Higher Consciousness communicates with human consciousness—spiritual coding. *Radical Light!* Descriptions and definitions of Light are more in alignment with higher physics than with occult beliefs. "Light" is more than just a spiritual catch-word. It is Light—it is just what it is.

In terms of the ego, the ego is programmed to recognize certain *frequencies* of information as Me, or Mine, and it guards this me, mine identity. Higher frequencies of information (Luminous Frequencies of Radiant Light), if they are unfamiliar to the ego, are resisted *as unknown outside and possibly dangerous others.* The first time your heart longs for truth, this longing begins to attract the Radical Light of Truth and the ego often resists the unfamiliar frequency.

This is why we repeat over and over, practices that support our heart's longing and we repeat those practices until the ego incorporates a body of experiences having to do with receiving these higher forms of communication—the ego begins to welcome Light as its own experience—and you experience anything from deep relaxation to bliss as your whole being responds to the Light of Knowledge and Wisdom—and you experience the exchange of Higher Information being received by your cells—and eventually by your own DNA.

Not only can the brain be transmuted, the DNA code can be transmuted.

Let's get back to beliefs. Which, by the way, become encoded into our DNA if we carry them through countless lifetimes. It's interesting to consider that each person's deep personal system of beliefs helps to give a unique form to each human being. And it is difficult to interpret what a belief is and even easily access what our individual beliefs are but at a deep emotional level we are always "charged" to defend the personal belief system we carry. Even if we can't articulate them or don't know what they are we feel the effect of our deep unconscious systems of belief.

Student: *"Would you say that you teach from a rigid set of beliefs? You must believe what you teach and sometimes the ideas seem rigid. Although each class you teach seems different from the other classes of the same genre. Do you create classes based on a rigid outline of beliefs? I don't know if I am making sense. I'm not sure what I am asking."*

You are mixed up about the difference between a *principle*—which is something that is practiced and a *belief*—which is something you believe in. Beliefs are powerful energies and the nature of beliefs is evangelical—you want to spread the word, you want to be sure everyone you know is on the same page as you are, so you naturally look for people you can enlist in your system, looking for true believers to bond with and create safety with. The nature of belief is that beliefs are either/or—such as; if you are not with me you are against me. There are strong conditions around each belief. Especially the condition that if everyone gathers together around the same belief system, you will all be truly safe.

A *principle* is something you practice. A principle has to do with what works; tried and true cause and effect. Most esoteric laws of energy are principles. For example, *if you practice such and such a principle, such and such will happen.* I teach principles and facts that would be defined as a technology rather than beliefs. There are facts that are true and there are principles that when applied work. And these are what I teach. If you diligently apply these esoteric principles, something happens.

I teach ancient principles that will work if you apply them diligently—you don't have to believe them, it doesn't matter if you believe them or not—but they do have to be practiced—just apply them. This is why I emphasize "DO YOUR PRACTICES!" If you don't apply these principles as practices, they won't work—and if they don't work, that is not about me it is about you and your resistance.

But as much as I love and respect these teachings, I am what you would call a devotee—I'm not a true believer. If I did teach from beliefs—if I functioned in this way, my mind would work in a much more theoretical way and I would spend a lot of class time trying to explain the concepts, turn them into theories, and analyze *why* you should believe the theories. I would analyze and study the ideas rather than emphasize "do the practices." I would be teaching you to interpret the world according to the belief rather than intuit the world according to your true experience.

I don't do that. I don't explain and I don't theorize or tell you what might happen or what is supposed to happen or why it happens. I have a general sense of the movement of each Class itself and I follow some kind of intuitive organic knowing, but I don't really plan each class lecture.

In your process through the Real Magic Course, you are not asked to believe anything I tell you, you are given techniques and principles to practice. If you diligently practice the principles, you will have experiences and you will believe your own experience and this—your own experience—will create a Path of Light and a spiritual Way of Life for you.

Student: *"This might not make sense but I have always wondered why you call your individual counseling sessions and teachings "readings"? Isn't this what the more occult teachers call what they do? Would you claim that you follow an occult lineage? Isn't that a belief?"*

OK, the individual counseling and teaching sessions that I call "readings"—I call them that because they are in the moment—I am *reading the moment* for the best available Guidance in each moment. So we, you and I, are participating in a moment in time and my job in that moment is to focus on Wisdom and on receiving Guidance from a Divine Source and make that focus available to you. This is why sometimes your sessions seem so different from time to time and even seem to contradict each other—each time, we are in a particular moment and the past has no bearing on that moment. *Reading* is the word that I think best describes being in the spiritual moment—it is an appropriate spiritual word, that's all.

Sometimes I'll have a sense of how an individual session or a class wants to go—or I'll receive key words from Guidance before I come to class. And then the class will go in that direction and it is really wonderful to watch it go in that direction—guided by a group spiritual superconsciousness just as your individual readings are Guided by your individual superconsciousness. But I don't have any set beliefs or rules or plans that I follow either way.

There is nothing in the Course that has to be taught or learned from a center of belief—and there is nothing to debate because there are no theories—there is nothing you are expected to believe. This is why it is so difficult to talk about the Real Magic Course to people who have not had the experience themselves of doing these practices—people who are used to the psychological methods of *talk about*—analyze and debate and discuss and theorize won't relate easily to these teachings. In this Course it is not possible to substitute a theory for real life. In this Course you experience your real life.

Your autonomy, your truth, your freedom, has to be experienced—it can't be debated and interpreted—this is why I ask you not to debate the Course, there is nothing to debate. And I ask you not to distract yourself with exploration into other practices. And especially don't compare the practices and teachings to other systems. There is nothing in your own experience that can be compared to another person's experience. It can only be experienced by you in your own unique way and then you will know freedom—and this freedom can only be experienced *if you do the practices!*

And by practices, I mean the Real Magic practices—but I do not mean *only* the Real Magic practices. A spiritual practice is determined by the Intention that lives in your heart—this is your true teacher and guide. This is the beauty of diversity, each one of us is so different, has such a different configuration, and we interpret the Course from our true nature as it emerges into life, rather than interpreting it from what we're told to believe about the Course. So each of you who takes the Real Magic Course does the same practices but each one of your experiences will be unique and true to you. If you are seriously attracted to meditations or techniques from other Courses and other teachers, then practice your autonomy and check these out, don't close your heart to anything. But don't bring your explorations into your Course classes—they are a distraction. And this practice of focusing on the teachings and practices in the Course sounds like a rigid system—until you experience the freedom involved. And your freedom comes as you experience revelations about Who You Are, which comes from your own experiences as you stay focused on the practices. So if you are not staying focused on the practices you close your heart. If you close your heart to your own experiences you will not receive revelations about Who You Are.

On the other hand, the practices when followed diligently and in a committed way, don't need any further study and comparison with other disciplines. All this does is distract you from your own experience and prevent you from directly experiencing Truth—because Truth resides in your own revelations about your Self, not in an intellectual inquiry into comparative systems. Self-knowledge comes from practicing self-inquiry which is opened for you by practicing the Course correctly. This is why I ask you to let go of comparing and debating and distracting yourself with intellectual systems and comparative systems.

Student: *"Speaking of practices, I have found that doing the meditation practices really accelerates my changes. And you say if there is a meditation we like, to add it to a daily practice. It seems to me that there many different types of meditations—and how do we know which ones are best? I do some breathing practices and sometimes I sit quiet and open to receive clarity about questions I have. Are there reasons why meditations are different? I know you have talked about active meditation and passive meditation—and Eastern religions teach a more passive approach. How much information do we need? Or do we need any? And what was my question . . . . ?" (laughter)*

Breathing practices to quiet brain and body are a universal practice—you can't go wrong with conscious breathing. And quiet receptivity is what meditation is about—be still and listen—meditation is about listening, about being enfolded in the Source of Grace.

And I do say if there is a meditation you especially like add it to your practices—just make sure you continue to do the RM practices and give them priority.

To be specific I would call the meditations we do in the Real Magic Course *active* meditations because they serve some specific purpose. They are *working* meditations. They allow your consciousness to work in specific ways—as in work-out—and to work out in ways that consciously stretch and change the brain. There is a lot of intentional and high frequency energy in something like the Focusing meditation. They are very intentional and during the Path of the Course are constantly and gradually raising your vibration—if you do the practices in a structured and intentional way—until you reach the practice of Superconscious Communion.

Passive meditation is not truly passive. The word has to do with the intention in the meditations. They are not generally focused on learning a new thought process and consciously being in the world in a new way. They are focused on stillness, on quieting and emptying the mind. They are not "Guided" in the way that a working meditation is but in essence there is not a significant difference between different forms of meditation. The essence of all meditation is stillness and Light. The essence of all spiritual practice is "Know Thyself".

In the truest sense all meditations move toward self-knowledge and unity because if they are practiced in a true way they lead to connection with the Source of Grace. And that means connection with the ultimate and authentic Self—Buddha Self or Christ Self or Atman or Allah—Self is one and the same whatever religion or system of meditation you practice. Your experiences will be determined by the intention within you to experience who you are.

And it is pretty much established by scientific experimentation that meditation awakens and utilizes parts of the brain that integrate the left and right brains. This promotes wholeness and healing. Spiritual practices change the structure of the brain in ways that allow us to experience the simplicity of wholeness. And we discover that meditation is really very simple. We complicate it with our notions about it—but it has nothing to do with our ideas about it. The simplicity of meditation escapes us because our convoluted ego-think wants to interpret and find the best "technique" that can help us learn something that really is unlearnable—something that Krishnamurti called the greatest *natural* art in life. He goes on to say it is a great natural art because we cannot learn it from anyone. That is the beauty of it—it has no technique and therefore no one has the center on what and how it is or the "right" way to do it.

It really is a kind of natural art—like loving the natural world in the stillness of dawn or being stunned by the first star to appear at twilight. Love stops the interpretive mind. Meditation is about Deep, Deep, Conscious Love and one of the best things about the meditative state is that the interpretive mind is stilled so that whatever we experience is in the moment and we experience it fully. It is our own true experience. In meditation we experience reality without the ego's drive to interpret and define it as an *experience*. This is true meditation, to experience the Silence of the Christ or the Silence of the Source directly.

But the meditations in the Course are specific and to do the Course in the most real and productive way, the meditations must be practiced in a constant and disciplined way. If passive meditation pulls you away from the Course meditations then please stop the passive meditation, stop doing other meditations until you have completed the Course. Too often the ego becomes accustomed to meditation as a 'feel good' and the Course meditations are hard work. Don't let a 'feel good' practice or an intellectual diversion distract you from The Great Work.

Student: *"Could you talk about the Law of Definition. Isn't that a belief?"*

No. The Law of Definition is a *principle* that is very workable. If you apply it, it works. If you apply it to your beliefs it works. You could make a belief about it but that would defeat the purpose of using it as a principle of application—a principle that when applied, works!

Soooo . . . What is the Law of Definition? Somebody tell me what the Law of Definition is. *(Silence.)* What is the Law?

Student: *"Well, you . . . define what's created. . . . what receives the most focus and attention is what's created . . ."*

That's true. You define something and give it attention, and it manifests. When something happens to you, you define it, pay attention to the definition, and re-create it. And I want to talk about that in a minute but first—what is the Law?

The Law of Definition is a law. It states this: *"Whatever definition in your consciousness is most prevalent—whatever you think about most—and this means both your subconscious thought and your conscious thinking—what you dwell on and consistently loop back to—will manifest into a tangible reality in your life."* Which means a thought will find expression and form in your environment *if it is given enough attention.* It is called Definition because it is the Law of the Word. When you define something it is a word that has impact and that word stays in your thoughts, your conscious or unconscious thoughts. And if you dwell on that definition, in your conscious thinking or unconscious thoughts, that definition will begin to manifest in your life.

It doesn't matter if it is a conscious or unconscious thought, if you dwell on a thought subconsciously you are still giving it tons of attention and that attention is what will keep it alive, energize it toward manifesting in some form. Why is that difficult to grasp? It is not even an abstract concept; it is an absolutely literal, absolutely concrete, simple law.

For example, something happens to you. If that something has *emotional impact*, you are going to *define it*, tell yourself what happened, describe it to yourself, tell your friends, talk about it. And if it had a strong enough emotional impact, this creates more and more reaction, so this definition is going to stay in your consciousness. It gets imprinted by our emotional response—the level of emotion is what really imprints our definitions into our consciousness.

So something happens, you define it, if there is not a strong emotional response, the definition dissipates. If there is a strong emotional response, the definition will stay around, allowing you to think about it, talk to your friends about it, imprinting the definition, and then you get attached to that definition, it comes to *mean* something to you, it gets attached like the peptides that attach to receptor cells in your brain, attached to other definitions in the same neural program, attaches to similar belief clusters, and becomes part of your belief system. It will encourage and support your existing beliefs. And all this gives you a deeply entrenched world view.

If it's a new definition, then you repeat it a lot, (mantra) and by repeating it a lot you insure that it becomes incorporated—entered into your existing program. In the practice and principles of Real Magic, the point of the Law of Definition is that every definition—every word that you have defined—that receives distinct, focused attention—(remember, attention is energy)—from you is going to manifest—it becomes part of your reality. Therefore *because of this Law,* you can consciously define and manifest a new existence.

Yes. This law of energy is the reason why if you create a definition and put it as a mantra at point B, and give it a lot of your attention—through the mantra—that definition at point B will manifest. Why? Because it is a universal Law of Creation. The Law became listed in the archives as a law because it is defining the workings of a universal principle.

I choose to receive blessing! Give this mantra a repeated and passionate *(I mean it!)* kind of attention and it will manifest. And if you create it as part of a polarity, (such as A=I feel cursed. B=I choose to receive blessing), then Point A (feeling cursed) is going to start dissipating—releasing from your consciousness. Every time you remember and focus on your point B definition, your point A definition will release even more and finally cease to exist. And Blessing will become more and more easily recognized. "Let me be surprised but let me know it's you."

Student: *"Could you draw the polarity as an energy map?"*

Yes. Remember this from Real Magic 101, class 1. I will draw this same drawing.

POINT A (let go here)	POINT B (focus attention here)
Depression	Joy, Serenity, Confidence
Trash	Treasure
Coal	Diamond
Pain	Wisdom
Old Reality	New Existence

There is your map—it gives a clear direction. Pull your attention out of Point A, let go. Allow your attention to follow the arrows to Point B. Then keep your attention focused at Point B. What could be clearer?

This is it, the Law of Definition, whatever you define and give the most attention to is going to come into being in some way or another in your life. What are the other laws that give vitality to this map? Go back to Chapter One and see if you can relate each law to your actual work with these Practices and Principles.

THE MOST RECOGNIZABLE OR IMPORTANT LAWS FOR OUR PURPOSES ARE:

The Law of Polarity—creates an energy map of Point A and Point B. This gives you direction and creates the alchemical vessel where all the energies of Creation can be contained and do their work.

The Law of Reversal—constantly and *consistently* reverse your attention away from Point A and shift the focus of your attention to your Intention at point B

The Law of Words of Power—create a mantra that expresses in a few words the Intention you have defined and are holding at Point B. Call that mantra often—give it Attention.

The Law of Repetition and *The Law of The Word* and *The Law of Attention, or, a thing becomes what it is repeatedly called*—helps you maintain the Energy you are creating and *contain* it at Point B. Everytime you call that mantra you are building a tremendous amount of energy at Point B. This is like putting money in a savings account in the bank.

The Law of Dissipation—if you don't want it don't feed it and it will dissolve, disappear because you are giving it no attention. This allows the letting go of the old energy of Point A.

What else is going on? *The Law of Magnetism* contained in the Law of Polarity will hold on to the energy that you are focusing toward Point B and keep that energy from leaking away. *The Law of Vibration* and *The Law of Attraction* will work within the vessel created by the Law of Polarity to attract even more energy that vibrates toward and merges with the energy you have already directed toward—and are holding on to at—Point B. This strengthens the Intention at Point B.

And you don't have to know anything about these laws. You don't have to know *anything* about any of this. All you have to know is the simple truth of your longing for a good life. All you have to do is follow the directions laid out for us by Hermes. Do the Practices! Maintain this energy in the vessel of your Polarity and the energy of Point B will become unmistakably real in your life and Point A will dissipate and disappear from your life. And in this creative process you will learn absolutely wonderful things about yourself. You will attain Self-Knowledge, the greatest gift it is possible to receive in any lifetime on any planet. *Know Thyself is the Eternal Commandment.* This is *Magic; the Simple Truth.*

CHAPTER EIGHT
EVOCATIVE QUESTIONS FROM PRIVATE SESSIONS

The questions in these chapters were asked by clients in private sessions. I would jot them down in a notebook because I often used these questions as inspiration for class teachings. I didn't always answer these questions in a private session the way I answer them here. Here I use them as teaching tools. I try to stay with the spirit of the student's question and some of them are word for word, but in most cases my answer is more extensive and less personal than it might have been in a private session.

Student Question: "What is Soul? Is it a true part of our being or just a religious idea? How do I know if I have experienced my Soul and is it even possible to experience one's Soul? It seems like such a vague and abstract religious idea—and unreal in terms of daily life."

Yes of course it is possible and yes, it is a true aspect of our being, in fact it is the truest aspect of Being. I once received, in a deep meditation, a superconscious transmission which included a description of being true to oneself. "*Feeling oneself as an immovable stillness, a Presence fluid, of a constant serenity; responsive to beauty, responsive to truth, but not existing in any definition of beauty or truth; a feeling not of identity, but of Beingness, rich, awake, and utterly Real.*" This description of being true to yourself is a description of experiencing one's Soul. This is what it feels like to feel one's Soul.

I also received this transmission about Soul: "*In wholeness. In silence. Only in deep and profound silence can one experience Soul. A deep, profound, feeling of stillness and silence is your Soul sensing Reality.*

There is nothing intellectual in it, nothing interpretive, it is the Silence of pure Knowing. Soul is an unpolarized whole, the Totality of your Self. Soul is the unpolarized essence of oneself just as God is the unpolarized Essence of Infinity. Soul is your capacity to feel God. To feel what God is. Soul is the sense organ of Infinity."

I believe that Soul is so deep, so beyond our human ability to conceive of, that it will take a lot more human experience of what is *not* true before humans can access that depth of truth that is our Soul. Soul is beyond any human interaction; it is where we are God. We are just beginning to study the superconscious mind—scientists are speculating about a "quantum mind" and when I first began teaching about the superconscious I called it our "big" mind (and I learned recently in Salt Lake City there is a Zen teacher who uses this phrase "Big Mind" to refer to our access to a higher mind within us). I think as we come to understand this aspect of our actual brain—as we learn the workings of our brain—we will move past brain/mind into that which constitutes 'soul'.

Student Question: "Could you define what you mean by Superconscious Guidance?"

Personally for me, it is a sense of vast intelligence, love, and wisdom that exists as Presence and has been with me all my life. When I was receiving transmitted Guidance about teaching, it began to refer to itself as Superconsciousness which I knew as the Christ Consciousness in the Esoteric Teachings and it often referred to Jesus or Sophia as the Christ Consciousness.

It is a shortcut word, an abbreviation. It refers to the experience of communion with Presence, with the Christ Consciousness. This often comes for me as an experience of Jesus or Sophia but not as if they had personality, the communion comes in a sense of Mindful Presence. I experience it as a vast and highly intelligent, all-encompassing, all-embracing essence of Light and Knowledge and Wisdom that is felt as an abiding Love—the All That Is. I received my definition of it from my own experience of Sophia and Jesus, from the definition of the Christ Consciousness in the Western Esoteric Tradition, from reading Yogananda and Aurobindo, and from deep meditation—from the energy itself, while I was in a deep meditative, intimate and highly conscious state of being.

In my first conscious transmission—by this I mean my first sense of deep awareness while fully conscious of a higher intelligence *communing with me*—It declared (roared), *"I am the Voice of Consciousness Itself"*—I still have the goose bumps.

The word, *superconscious*, according to Yogananda and Aurobindo, refers to both the highest frequency that human consciousness can reach and the God-spark, or point, where human consciousness merges and communes with Cosmic Consciousness. In his book *Autobiography of a Yoga*, Yogananda speaks very beautifully and intimately about the Superconscious as a highly evolved and deeply intimate experiencing of Truth. In Aurobindo's writings, he refers it as the evolution of the human mind and brain.

Same Student Question: "Thank you. Is it possible for the ego to experience the Soul."

Certainly. This is the goal of all human experience, for the ego to know Soul. The ego is a part of our whole consciousness and being consciousness, it is energy, and being energy, it has the capacity to expand and shift, to *change and expand its awareness.* When you experience wholeness it is an indication that your egoic consciousness has merged with your greater conscious awareness. The ego, because it acts like a *preservative*, seeks to preserve your identity as it knows it, as it exists in present time. Ego does not seek to explore what does not exist. If the ego was an explorative consciousness rather than a preservative, you would be unable to retain an identity, your sense of self would be constantly changing. When the explorative parts of your consciousness have explored a new experience and repeatedly defined the experience over and over, the new experience will be accepted by the egoic part of your consciousness, and incorporated as part of your identity. Then, your ego will preserve the new identity, the new expression of who you are. If the explorative parts of your consciousness are exploring Soul with a deep longing, Soul will be experienced gradually and at many levels until the ego accepts Soul as part of your identity and you experience 'Soul'.

Student Question: "What do you mean by saying 'don't take rage personally'? I would like to know how to do that—how can rage not be taken personally!?"

A general rule in transformation is *"accept everything but don't take anything personally."* And this holds true for all of the most intense and seemingly overwhelming emotions such as rage.

We are taught that violent emotion is powerful. It can even seem exciting to believe that one has a 'deep rage' imbedded in one's psyche as part of one's identity—but the truth is that the rage you feel is not your rage, so it is pointless to try to use it as an excuse for not being true to yourself. Rage is part of the dynamic of the ego and you can refer that back to the equality of the ego. *All egos are equal in the moment of expression.* If your ego is expressing rage it just means that rage is one of the many forms of expression *easily* available to *all egos*, and if you choose to allow the *collective rage* that your ego is expressing into your personal *identity,* (i.e. take it personally) and allow it any importance, if you look for meaning in it, give it meaning, you may do so but it does not serve any useful purpose and you might find yourself trapped in addiction to it. *It is only a choice* and if you express it, this simply means that you are choosing to make yourself available to the energy of rage and you choose to express that rage.

I remember going through a period of reading articles on spiritual teachers. I was looking for guidance about how I was supposed to be. I read in many of the new spiritual journals coming out that many Zen and Buddhist teachers would fly into rages at their students, even hit them. I found this shocking and asked for Christ Guidance on this. What I received was that even a spiritual teacher can call on rage as a teaching tool when they need to severely shake up a student's ego. They simply make themselves available to rage and it flows through them in appropriate ways. This gave me a whole new take on collective emotional energies. It goes something like this:

You are making yourself available to rage and you will receive (and project) whatever you make yourself available to. So it is best to know what you are making yourself available to and what you choose to do with it.

I have experienced this as what I call "the roar" sometimes coming at me, sometimes coming through me to a student. And when that happens I have felt something I can describe as irritated at a student except that it never feels personal and never stays, it passes very quickly, and when it passes through it is gone and I never lose sight of my focus as "Teacher."

Taking it personally means you are claiming it as your own, being a victim in the face of it, being available to it rather than making it a point A choice and transmuting it into a quality that truly resonates. *You.* This availability to the energy of rage—or to any of the collective ego-centric emotions—feeds your self-importance and is one of the ways the ego finds to distract you from Reality. Reality being the fact that you are your Authentic, True, Self and nothing can harm that Self. Rage is not and cannot be a part of Who You Are. This is beyond choice. Reality is the part of truth that is beyond rage. Reality is "who you are".

Rage, on the other hand, is a choice you are making and has nothing to do with who you are. This is true of all the "deep psyche" emotions—they are collective, available to all egos and available all the time, any time, to any ego, *but they are not Reality*. Rage does not constitute Reality. By Reality we refer to the fact that the true nature of the Self is joy and the true expression of the Self is love. Truth is ecstatic. The Soul is not available to these collective attachments—it cannot feel the emotion of "rage".

Teacher's Comment: *This question was asked in a private session and it was hard for this person to hear because she was in therapy and deep in a belief that she had the right to hold on to and feel her anger as a healing tool. I told her yes, she did have some things to be angry about and she had the right to choose to stay angry, but there is never a good reason to retain, hold on to, or justify anger. She agreed that this is a very sane approach to anger but she chose to stay angry!*

She made that choice to stay angry with so much humor, feeling the absurdity of it, that it very quickly nullified her anger. How can you hold on to anger if you burst out laughing every time you experience the feeling of anger and refer to it as a slightly absurd choice you are making? We take anger much too seriously. We should emulate Crazy Wisdom and laugh at the absurdity of it.

There is also a difference in the frequency of outrage. This emotion is very different from the projection that we refer to as "rage". Outrage can be a healthy response to something that is genuinely unjust or wrong, like racism, or violence against animals, children, people, or the earth. If we can learn to temper righteous outrage against injustice with wisdom we can truly be a force for change.

Same student: "But what about the kind of mental illness that is characterized by uncontrollable rage? Some brain damaged people have uncontrollable rage. And what about steroid-induced rage? Is this caused by collective rage?"

Well, look at it this way—what if rage did not exist as a collective emotion that could find expression through human chemical/hormonal reactions? What if rage was not available? Rage is a collective energy that is ego-centered no matter what chemical is used to create the uncontrollable expression of it. What do you think causes a mob to act so violently? People do atrocious things in a group that they would be unwilling to do as individuals. We know from studying the brain that rage has its origin in the limbic system; the so-called reptile or "old" brain. I don't think there are any studies of the brain and emotion that include the study of alchemy and the use of the Hermetic laws to transmute rage. I think such transmutation is possible but it will be a long time coming. We have so little information about the brain and how it functions. Right now we are learning to change this person-by-person by choosing consciousness.

We are learning now at a collective level that thought can change brain patterns, which would indicate that the conscious use of thought can affect matter and that would include the transmutation of chemicals. But until some wise person undertakes a scientific, laboratory structured study of how thought affects brain chemistry, we will be subject to these archaic ideas and superstitions about emotion. There is, though, more and more studying of emotion and the brain being undertaken by scientists and I think the day is coming when, besides chemical treatment, healing of the brain will include technologies like Real Magic.

Same Student: "You just mentioned "the equality of the ego." What do you mean by equality of the ego?"

This simply means that cruelty is cruelty, meanness is meanness, jealousy is jealousy, anger is anger, competition is competition, pettiness is pettiness—it means that there are no greater or lesser degrees of these patterns that can make them—cruelty, meanness, jealousy, anger, competition, pettiness, etc—more or less acceptable—these are all indications that the ego is fully engaged, totally involved in an available collective thought form.

This is equality—there is no such thing as the ego being just a little bit involved, the nature of ego is to be *totally* involved in your identity and all egos are equal in this expression of identity. It does not matter if one is an axe murderer or simply projecting angry or murderous thoughts toward another, in that moment the ego is totally engaged in self-preservation and all egos are equal in this—and murder, whether as a projected thought or a physical action, is equal—one and the same.

So many killers now are children—they don't distinguish between the feeling, the idea, the urge, and the action. They are functioning as pure egoic self preservation according to their reality and their solution is to eliminate the source of their pain and anger. It is a truly terrible way to have to learn accountability and the reality of consequences.

The ego is a consciousness within you and its function is self-preservation. All egos have one equal function—*self-preservation*—to keep the identity intact, safe. This is the equality of the ego. We all have this function to some degree.

Don't think that the prevalence of war and hatred on this planet is not influencing every being. This is a collective call that pulls at everyone who has an ego. Our biggest job or purpose as human beings is to look at this larger picture and commit to transmuting the beliefs that create war and hatred, any impulse toward violence; any focus on "dangerous others" within ourselves. As transformed Beings we can create a new planet.

Same Student: "Then why aren't we all murdering each other equally? And if you, being a spiritual teacher, have an ego, what keeps you from taking an axe to people who ask you stupid questions?"

(I told this man that there is no such thing as a stupid question!)

Each person is different and the same because of what the ego is preserving. The ego is preserving something called "identity". If your "identity" does not include the belief (or the desire) that you have the *right* to take an axe to anyone who bothers you with stupid questions—*(which, of course, means questions that you can't answer)*—then, even if you have the feeling of anger, it will not be an idea which becomes an action—you will not commit physical murder.

Nothing can make you physically take an axe to another human being if the permission to do so is not part of your identity and alive somewhere in some part of your consciousness. If you cannot envision yourself doing it, you will not commit the actual physical action. And this is the danger of video and TV violence. The person observing the image identifies with the image and if their consciousness is not strong and well formed, they will have no hesitation or remorse about killing. It is just an image, not flesh and blood.

This inability to commit physical murder is the first step toward being unpolarized, or, unconditional being—but—the mental ego separates the thought from the deed and most people believe it is all right to murder others if it is done "only" as a movie, as "entertainment," *only* as an angry or obsessive thought they are projecting and not a "real" event. True freedom and unpolarized love can only manifest when a person is no longer capable of killing another in any capacity—mentally, emotionally (as a projection), or physically. And when human forms of entertainment do not include the torture and death of living beings.

Most people are quick to anger when it comes to preserving their egoic self-interest. If you ever have an angry, self-righteous thought projected as a judgment toward someone, a desire to get even, to prove someone wrong, to prove that you are more right or better than someone, a belief that your anger is justified or your envy is justified because you feel threatened—if you are, at some level, seeking to destroy what you have defined as a threat against you or if you are falsely accusing another because of racial or gender or religious differences, then you are what Jesus defined as "carrying a murderer in one's heart."

CHAPTER NINE
EVOCATIVE QUESTIONS FROM PRIVATE SESSIONS

S tudent Question: "What is competition? Why is it frowned on by spiritual teachers? What is so bad about it? Doesn't it encourage excellence?"

Competition is a distraction from Reality. The moment you create an "either/or" or a "winner/loser" you have division and division creates separation within yourself. Competition, rather than encouraging excellence, perpetuates separation because the division of one side being better than another side or one side having to win and one side having to lose is an exercise that strengthens the egocentric belief that separation is a valid solution to problems.

This state of separation leads to aggression around the either/or mind set. Competition requires a belief that the winner is better than the loser, and winning deserves a reward. And it encourages a mockery of qualities like trust and empathy. In competition the only thing important is winning. Competition rather than encouraging excellence, encourages beliefs in lack and scarcity and the belief that self-preservation and maintaining the status quo is more valid than the pursuit of a conscious life. Therefore it is a distraction from Reality.

The desire for excellence can come from a respect for integrity and a desire to be true to oneself, to always do one's best. This does not require any competition.

Student Question: "You often refer to one-way bargains as "hallucination". I 'get' that obsession is something you project and is often a fantasy—and it's a reality and scenario that the object of your fantasies doesn't know about, but which you believe is actually happening—but could you explain the hallucination part of one-way bargains. I'm not sure of what you mean by one-way bargain?"

A hallucination is something conjured up in your thoughts—the hallucination part is that you believe that something that is basically a thought-form, conjured up in your own thoughts and your own fantasy—is true and actually happening in the outside world. A visual hallucination is when you actually *see* forms and colors. An audio hallucination is when you actually *hear* sounds.

A one-way bargain refers to agreements that you have made concerning another person that the other person isn't aware of. It has to do with the expectation that if you conduct yourself in certain ways, the other person will reward you by meeting your conditions. Unfortunately, the other person is not aware of this hidden agenda, your unspoken bargain with them. And when that other person doesn't act in ways that fulfill your expectations you feel hurt, offended and angry with them and blame, attack and punish them in some way. This form of hallucination is very prevalent in this third-dimensional, psychological/emotional, world. Being in love often carries many one-way bargains. The phenomenon of stalkers is an extreme form of one-way bargain.

The concept of a one-way bargain is used often in therapy. I first heard the phrase in a workshop on unconditional love and to illustrate this kind of illusory agreement, the teacher used the parable of the prodigal son from the teaching stories of Jesus. This was very exciting for me because The Prodigal Son was one of my favorite Jesus stories when I was a child—at least once a year my church gave a Sunday School class on the meaning of the parable of the Prodigal Son. The teachings in this story impacted and stayed with me all my life.

The story, as told by Jesus, is that there were two sons, a "good" son and a "bad" son. The good son did everything "right" assuming that if he did so, the father would reward him with love and approval and he would be the favored son. The good son tried to live up to what he assumed his father wanted and he tried to be better than the bad son.

The bad son quarreled with the father, left home, and lived a wild, selfish, decadent life. The good son stayed home and did everything according to his assumption that the father would reward him. The father had not discussed this with or made any agreement with either son. It was something the good son assumed because of what he wanted from the father. The good son had a one-way bargain with the father.

Years went by and the bad son was given up for lost. But one day the bad son appeared at his father's door destitute and ill. When the prodigal son returned home, poor and sick, the father wept for joy and called for a great feast. The good son went into a rage of disappointed expectations. He had done everything right and the father was supposed to reward him by rejecting and punishing the bad son.

The father had not agreed to this. The father did not know about the good son's one-way bargain. He hadn't agreed that if the good son was good he would be rewarded and part of that reward would be that the bad son would be rejected. The father wept for joy because his son who was lost had returned to him. The father received a miracle and celebrated.

The good son was focused on an illusory outcome. Outcome thinking goes hand in hand with one-way bargains. If you have a one-way bargain with someone, you are going to be very attached to what happens in your interactions with that person. If you act good and do the right thing and try to impress them and do this with the expectation of a reward from them, you will be rewarded with truth and truth might disappoint you. The other person will disappoint, offend and hurt you in countless ways because they are not aware that you have made a deal with them that says they must fulfill your conditions and expectations. They disappoint your expectations over and over and you react by projecting blame toward them for disappointing you. Then you try to manipulate them so they won't hurt and disappoint you again. You will obsess on all the things wrong with that person, go over and over your list of how much that person hurt you and how wrong and messed up that person is. Often you will react by confronting that person with a list of damages, the ways in which they have disappointed you. You will try to manipulate a deal or get them to sign a contract that will guarantee that they never again disappoint you. In the light of day it looks kind of crazy. It does not constitute sanity but it does pass for relationship in a large segment of human culture.

One-way bargains are a human creation. God does not make deals or sign contracts. In a passage from the spiritual teacher Ama, where she is describing her version of making "deals" with God, she says that the ego is the only offering God asks of us. And she says if you are not willing to surrender your ego once God has asked, then it will be taken from you.

Your true deal with Creation is your agreement to be true to yourself. That is why I say your conscious choices constitute an agreement with God. *Choice is a sacred agreement* but Creation cannot make your choices for you—Creation simply honors your choices and says 'yes' to whatever choice you make. You are free to choose your path toward Truth. Freedom is in your relationship with Truth and Truth does not make deals or sign contracts. Truth just appears and blows all illusions, expectations, assumptions, false beliefs, and one-way bargains, out of the water. Look at your life. How many times in your life have you made a one-way bargain with others and been disappointed? When you hang on to disappointment and suffering, hang on to outcomes you thought should have happened, hang on to the feeling that someone owes you something, and hang on to your list of damages, you are often reacting to one-way bargains that you yourself have created. Let go of illusions about what you need from others and about how others should be and what the outcomes in your life should be. What do you *really* want? Be honest with yourself. Your truest outcome is Freedom.

Student Question: "What is the most important thing to think about—or the best approach to—power points? How would you tell a new student to approach it? What is the point of power points?"

It is always to your advantage to polarize the energy of your conflict. This gives you a clear understanding of the forces at work in a power point. Actually writing it out as A and B gives you a map of the direction you want your attention to take. This helps your attention to stay on Point B.

This polarized structure allows you to create a powerful creative *tension* that is crucial if change is going to manifest. This is more creative and more effective than trying to violently force contradictions into an either/or decision. And this is much less violent and energy wasting than trying to make yourself forcefully quit some habit or pattern you are attached to.

For example, in a consciously created polarity there are no energy drains—energy doesn't drain away from the starting point or leak away from the fulfillment point. Opposing and even contradictory poles of thought can create between them a *conscious* creative tension that resolves itself into a new form. In order for this to happen, a tremendous amount of *contained* (as in container) energy is needed. Therefore you want to gather and concentrate as much energy as you possibly can in the easiest and most effective way. A consciously created polarized structure allows you to contain tremendous amounts of energy *easily* and *effectively and move that energy in the direction you want it to go.*

And this is the purpose of a power point—it is an opportunity to powerfully move energy in the direction you want it to go in order to more effectively and quickly manifest the existence you want to create.

A power point is a point where your attention is overwhelmed by the energy of your destructive emotions or by your fear of contradictions when you are trying to make a choice. Stress (feelings of rage or weakness, hurt or pain) is usual in a power point. Self-protection is the action when you are in stress. The first reaction when you are stressed is to defend yourself and find your safety.

A new reaction we are learning is to look at a power point as an opportunity to work directly with the energy of unwanted emotion in the moment when you are *feeling the emotion*, rather than processing ideas and stories *about* the emotion long after the moment has passed. So in a power point you have a chance to *shift and transmute* the energy of emotion *at the moment* when you are *feeling* it (this is a good reason to *not* focus on the feeling.) Utilizing power points can accelerate your ability to manifest the kind of existence you want. Utilizing power points brings you into the moment. The best thing to tell yourself in a power point is that a chaotic and stressful emotion is just *energy doing things*. Ask yourself if chaos and stress is what you want your energy to be doing at that moment.

Practicing power points teaches you to live in the moment. It takes you away from making a project of "being in the moment" and moves you into simply being present now—as the moment is happening! A power point is a point where you take action in the "now". That is the "point" of a power point. Choose to master the moment.

Student Question: "Could you, or would you, clarify what you mean when you say things like 'Your feelings don't matter.' That really threw me into confusion. You say attention is the most powerful thing we have but I believe and most people I know believe that feelings are the most powerful thing we have."

Feelings *feel* powerful because of the chemical effect of emotions on our brain. They are similar to the effect that drugs have. But they are not any more powerful than drugs are. When the chemical of the feeling wears off, where is your power?

Most human beings come of age in an ego-centric, psychologically oriented, and emotionally manipulative world. We are taught that truth resides in our feelings. In the esoteric world, in the polarity of ego/soul, you learn a spiritual and creative orientation, and in this spiritual orientation, it is important to be aware of your feelings but not to regard them as truth. Your feelings are *energy doing things*. Your feelings are something you have that might have very little to do with who you really are. Your feelings are simply a message to you *that a belief has been activated.*

Please notice that I never say "*Ignore your feelings.*" That's right! I never tell you to ignore (or deny) your feelings. That is not what I am saying. Pay attention to your feelings, they are giving you important information about yourself, information about things you might want to change. But the feeling itself is not important and *processing* the feeling just makes it more difficult for you to *transmute* the feeling. The worst thing you can do, in terms of Real Magic is to hang on to your victim identity—don't stay with any hurt or offended feelings that arise in you when I make statements like that. These statements are designed to invoke a deeper self-inquiry and a deeper inner quest within you. A quest for Who You Are.

In practice, *notice* your feelings without taking them *personally*. Above all do not obsess on hurt feelings (victim) or project blame and do not make other people responsible for care-taking your feelings. Don't do that. Let go of victim and choose to have all your relationships be about truth and grace. Your feelings don't matter—the truth of who you are matters. The polarity of (A) your feelings vs. (B) who you are, is a gateway to wisdom and self-knowledge.

You could say that the most important and powerful feeling you will ever have is the feeling of joy, even ecstasy, which comes from the manifest truth, serenity, and wisdom that follows true transformation.

CHAPTER TEN
EVOCATIVE QUESTIONS FROM PRIVATE SESSIONS

I used notes from working with this particular woman to actually create this chapter and some teaching about relationship for this book. This woman was highly intelligent and she married late in life. She was very spiritual and not willing to accept that he was just not available to the ideals she had tried to cultivate all her life. We had several counseling sessions before she discontinued work with me. She returned to work with me years later and had separated from her husband and was very happy and grateful. This was all done by telephone. I never met her in person but that was not relevant. She had an inquiring mind and asked many questions.

Student Question: "What exactly is meant by the word 'manifesting'? I try to do these practices but I keep running into a big 'Why'. Why should I or anyone do this work? What difference does being true to yourself make in this insane world?"

In its most literal and esoteric sense the verb *to manifest* means to bring something new into being. Alchemically it is the action of transmuting one vibration into another vibration and thus creating a new form.

A good reason to do this work is that it is much more rewarding and satisfying to be conscious and fearless and true than it is to be an unconscious person who is driven by fear and who lives in a state of anxiety and uncertainty in a world of chaos.

Being true to yourself means that as you transmute your old patterns, your belief system changes, you learn to believe in yourself in ways that support your highest intentions all the time. Serenity replaces anxiety and you exist in a new and different relationship with stress.

There are terrible things going on in the world and this makes us feel small and uncertain of who we are. We feel powerless to change anything. We look for some big, important, work to identify with and be involved in because we want to believe that we can be effective. We compare our lives to our social, cultural, and peer definitions of big and important and come to believe our personal dreams are unimportant. Organized religion supports this belief-oriented way of thinking because organized religion is based on being true to the belief rather than being true to oneself. This diminishes autonomy. We are encouraged socially, morally, and religiously to believe that wanting things for ourselves is selfish. This keeps us searching outside ourselves for a work we can identify with that is important, unselfish, prestigious, politically, and socially correct. This keeps us in a state of constantly comparing ourselves to what is "important". This does not help us discover our true being or our true work or the fulfillment that comes from being true.

Being true to yourself leads you into a state of being that is harmonious and peaceful. It is a state of being filled—filled with peace, grace, abundance, wisdom, joy—and when you are full you can't do anything but give and your giving is appropriate and powerful and effective. Doing a work like this teaches us to let go of projecting self-importance and gives us a path based on what is most important to us in a way that expresses our own integrity.

In a search for true autonomy you are constantly letting go of self-importance. Autonomy comes as you keep *choosing* to manifest the qualities that are most important to you. The world "choose" is vital to your freedom. The fact that you always have a choice is central to your autonomy and central to your relationship with your Self. When you declare your choice to be true to yourself, you are declaring that you want a conscious relationship with your world. The word choose immediately establishes a relationship of commitment between you and your world and your God. "I Choose" is a word of power that puts you in the position of creating and receiving in a conscious, responsible and powerful way. And this leads you to a way of life that is true to your Self. When being true to your Self becomes a constant way of thought because you have changed your own state of being, then you have effectively changed the world.

Same Student: "Then how would you apply these teachings in real life—in a relationship? This seems to be the hardest part of this work—it doesn't make sense when I try to apply it—it is just too hard and people don't understand it. Some people just don't want to change and they don't care about the world."

In that case this might not be the right work for you. You have a choice to make. No one *has* to want to change the world. That is not a requirement. But this work, if you continue it and live it in a constant way, *will change the world*. What do you want? Do you know? Can you tell me what it is you really want in your deepest truest heart?

Same Student: (she is weeping) "I know I want peace—I want to have a peaceful life."

Then these teachings and this work will create a world of inner peace for you. And imagine how you could bring everyone you love into this peace. How would you apply these teachings in a real life situation if you knew you could bring everyone you love into a peaceful life? And are you actually saying you want peace? Is it more accurate to say that you want safety. Well you can create true safety also.

How? Always respond to challenging relationships with a determination to be true to yourself and always ask yourself what it is you want to create in this relationship. Allow each power point to become, "What can I create now?" I know that you believe that truth means confrontation. It doesn't. Truth does not mean confronting the other with what you think is wrong in an attempt to fix the relationship. Truth is not something you confront. Truth is something you *receive* when you become more true to yourself. Create a Point A of conflict and a Point B of Blessing. Choose that your relationship with truth be a relationship based on blessing.

In most intimate relationships assume that you have issues based on *unconscious* agreements each of you have made with each other and which unconsciously include manipulation. These are *one-way bargains* you each have made about your safety and what you need to be safe. This kind of need that is focused on safety can turn the relationship into a power struggle, which keeps each of you focused on loss and damage and fear.

I know that you each spend a lot of energy evaluating damage and avoiding more damage. Each of you is struggling to control how the other reacts and get the reaction that will make you feel safe again. You are both unconsciously focused on safety.

You and your significant other can practice recognizing that you are in a mutual power point and treat your conflict as such. Talk to each other in a new way. Ask each other what it is you want in your relationship. What did you want to create by coming together in a relationship—this question in itself can make the relationship more conscious. Why do you suppose the two of you met, what kind of existence does your Soul want to create? Create blessing mantras for the relationship and when conflict comes up, stay with the mantras you create.

In a power point your old relationship patterns will try to exert through each of you. You might be tempted to explain yourself or demand explanations from them—bring up past damage and debate "who's right/who's wrong." Don't do this. Don't explain or second-guess yourself. Do not try to fix-it or debate it. Truth is not about debate. Ask each other "What does blessing mean to you?" and be prepared to actually listen to each other—you could even create a blessing list and turn it into a list of mutual mantras.

You can say to each other, "What can we let go of and what can we focus on as blessing in its place?" And, if you don't know, choose silence and wait. Don't try to make up something in an attempt to manipulate the moment. Truth can be silent. If you don't know what you want, stay silent. And by silence, I don't mean pouty, sulking, manipulative, or withholding kind of silence. I mean the Silence of the Christ.

If you are both *(in this case, they were both taking the Course but he had made it a dangerous other and was fighting it)* taking the Course, you can always do a meditation from the Course together. If you work the energy of conflict into a power point and choose mutual blessing and stay still, something creative will emerge. The important thing is that you don't ask the other person to make a project of your safety. At the same time, you don't agree to make their safety your project. *(She was doing this, making a project of his safety and comfort so that she could feel safe.)*

The greatest pain in relationships comes from withholding being true to yourself. You can't give truth when you are not in touch with truth. So don't make false promises trying to fix things. And don't judge truth—don't try to judge whether it is enough truth or is it the real truth or is it the whole truth. Do your best to be honest and open and give what you can—and sometimes all you can give is your silence, or tears, or your admission of how frightened you are of being hurt and how unsafe you are feeling. But do this without looking for blame. Let go of expectations that the other person is supposed to take care of you and fix it. You want to create something more true than an old idea of safety based on false evidence and manipulation. Surrender your ego. Give it up.

No judgments and no self-condemnation. No conditions on how you want truth to look. Truth appears and you can't manipulate it, you can only choose it and go forward with a good heart, choosing to trust truth. Don't judge truth according to your feelings. *Your feelings are not truth*. This moment is not about your feelings. It is about your quiet steadfast true self. It is about creating an even greater relationship with yourself. The best gift you can give to the world, and to your significant other, is to be true to yourself. When you are true to your own authentic heart and soul, you can't present a false appearance to anyone. And the truest practice toward truth is to look into each other's eyes (no matter how angry and hurt you are) and choose blessing for each other.

(He was unable to do this because he felt he was unable to let go of his own pain, anger, and blame)

So, how do you apply these teachings in your daily life? Be constant. All the time. Do your practices. Create sacred space, altars, ceremonies to remind yourself that every day, all the time, you want to live in a constant reality, a conscious, true, powerful, happy, and successful existence. No more marginal part-time existence.

Same Student: (She is still crying.) "Well, what if he is not willing to do any of those things? What if he feels threatened by my doing this?"

What to do if transformation is not a mutual desire? I am so sorry. I am not sorry for you, or sorry that you have this great opportunity in your life. I am sorry that so many people believe they can only be safe if they can control the content of their world. It sounds like he is afraid of loss and damage and wants to control your relationship so that he will be safe. Or he is afraid to be too open for fear of what might come in—rejection. I am not a marriage counselor. I am here to support your most important relationship. What is your most important relationship? Your relationship with yourself is the most important relationship you have. This is what I support.

You have to accept that he might be so afraid of truth that if you continue in the Work, he might leave you—or you might decide to leave him. You have to be courageous in your relationship with yourself. You have to make a choice. And since he is asking you to choose between this work and him, you have to remember that this is your life, these are your choices, and also that you can, if you feel you must, commit yourself and devote yourself to helping him feel safe. In this case, you might be telling yourself that compassion is more important than freedom?

Same Student: "Yes, I do . . . that is how I feel."

There is no blame to you if you let go of these practices and choose compassion. Compassion will come to you, it will come alive in you if you keep asking for it. But what is compassion? A key component of compassion is wisdom. And it might be that compassion will teach you that you are not helping him when you try to protect him from his fear. And compassion might bring you the revelation that the fear you are protecting is your own fear of loneliness. But whatever revelation comes to you, it must come through your relationship with yourself. And this is where you want to ask yourself what you can create that will most serve life. And you do not have to find this by taking this Course. This Course is just one way—it is not the only way. But do choose to know yourself. Wake up every morning with the willingness to know Who You Are.

Your relationship with your Self is a relationship with your Source. You might think of Source as God, or your Higher Self, or your Higher Power—whatever you call it, it is your connection with a Greater Intelligence, Wisdom, and Guidance beyond your daily hassles, it is your Source of Radiant Awareness and Divine Love. This is the most personal relationship you have. And you bring this relationship with yourself into every relationship you have.

Repeat that over and over: You are the only one who knows your relationship with your Self. No one can tell you Who You Are. No one can tell you what choices to make. This life, for you, is about learning to trust yourself. And this is your practice, choose to trust yourself and choose to trust Compassion. Choosing to trust yourself is a way of choosing to be true to yourself and that choice will lead you to be conscious of what you already know. Just trust that you know what, and you know why, and you know how—you know all of this about this relationship—you know truth. How do you want to walk? Walk with Love. Ask Compassion to Guide you.

Same Student: (smiling—she has stopped crying) "Thank you."

Same Student: "You say that if the word 'God' is hard for us that we can substitute the word 'Creation' instead. What is the meaning of these words? Why should we use either of them when we talk about manifesting? What is Creation when you use it in the context of this work? Why is it important? The world is insane."

(My answers to this woman are much longer in this book version but I have tried to stay true to her inquiry.)

What is it? It is a relationship. It is a relationship within which no one can ultimately ever truly fail. Call it God or Creation or Divinity; call it Higher Power, call it Presence, or the Source or the One or the All, it is a constant and original energy that exists as a constant state of being within us and around us and within all form and ultimately, at the end of each life, we return to this constant and original state of energy—we return to Source.

Your relationship with the Divine; with Creation, is the most powerful force in your life. Call it any Word you like, it is possible to have a rich, nurturing, loving, and conscious relationship with Creation. It would seem that this is something to be desired. Yet many people resist this relationship. Why is it resisted?

Your relationship with Creation has to do directly with *what you are willing to receive*. Resistance to receiving is usually because you are fixated on outcomes that are fueled by the beliefs you are carrying in your consciousness. If you have distorted expectations about life, or about a relationship, you will always be judging the outcome that *didn't* happen or which you believe was *supposed to* have happened or should have happened. This is like constantly asking God for proof that you are loved. God or some outside force has to prove that he loves you and make something happen. This creates a relationship of disappointment and victim with the Source. This keeps us living a marginal existence, in a constant state of disappointed expectation.

And a lot of disappointments happen when manifesting itself becomes a commodity. All the advertising leads us into thinking nothing's happening if our methods don't bring fast results or if an outcome doesn't happen the way we think it should happen. Here too you have a relationship of disappointed expectations with the Source.

And some people have such strong egos, are so psychologically/mentally programmed that something like an esoteric, path just isn't right for them—they just aren't ready for this kind of diving into the depths without a lifejacket. They can't function in an environment that asks for trust and faith but offers no proof. They need a different approach and this is not a fault or an indication that there is anything wrong with them or with esoteric teachings—it is just where they are at. Some people need therapy and processing. At any rate, whatever your relationship to the Source (or to the Course) whenever you catch yourself making judgments about what is or isn't happening in your life, stop and tell yourself that your expectations might be blocking your receiving.

Human beings are programmed to think of outcomes in terms of gratification and safety. It doesn't matter if the outcome is about your breakfast or about your transformation, it doesn't matter if it is about manifesting joy, truth, and beauty or about manifesting your worst fears—your interpretive ego is going to try to control the process and fit the outcome to your expectations. When you tell yourself over and over again to let go of outcomes, it is your *expectations* that ultimately let go. This is why it is so important to let go of trying to control outcomes and trying to control process—and why it is so important to choose patience.

What is patience? Patience is a quality. You can't know what patience is until you feel it within you, but you can know what patience creates. Patience creates certainty—deep certainty about life, and deep trust in divine order. It replaces anxiety as a state of being. Patience creates Faith.

Anxiety arises from the fear that an outcome won't come at all, or won't come in a way that will help you feel safe. The belief that you won't be safe unless you get the outcome you need keeps you attached to anxiety about outcomes and attached to *time as a limitation*. Where there is patience, time becomes limitless and a feeling of trust and certainty about outcomes comes into being. You know that your needs and wants are unfolding just as they ought, in a divine order. And age becomes meaningless.

The feeling of stress and of time running out is such a part of modern life that people don't question it. Modern culture programs us to either seek distraction from stress or search for ways to process and fix stress. We are not taught freedom. Instead of independence we have floating dependencies—dependencies that shift around and are not connected to real needs.

Look at the dependence on style and image in our culture, on having the right look or presentation, on the importance attached to impressing others, and the fear about what others will think. These standards and values are *programmed* needs—not *real*—not true and natural needs. These needs are perpetuated by the media and the entertainment industry—and even by the human potential industry. The rhetoric of the human potential industry often promotes greed in the same way the *old world* human political-industrial industry at the turn of the century promoted ripping off the planet in the name of evolution, of human destiny and progress.

The news media—even the new age and spiritual media—is focused on personalities and sensational stories, on marketing, and on success that is determined by quantity and not quality. This focus perpetuates celebrity worship and obsession with image. This accelerated sensationalism means that each new need comes with an increased anxiety level and an increased search for gratification. Increased emptiness, increased fear of lack, and increased anxiety about outcomes is the heritage we are creating through this kind of relationship with Creation.

As a species we have become adept at self-deception. Our greatest self-deception is the belief that some*thing*—like money, or the right partner, or enlightenment, or involvement with an important work or purpose, or involvement with the right teacher—will make us feel safe and fulfilled. People compulsively seek distraction from emptiness in a larger, more sensational experience and compulsively resist the spiritual practices that are designed to bring real fulfillment and real safety. Even in the spiritual market place people distract themselves with classes and workshops, it has become a way of life that adds to distraction all in the name of looking for one's purpose. This kind of thinking encourages the belief that we are separate from God and creates a relationship of alienation with Creation.

Creation as the Source of Consciousness is sentient, aware but impersonal. Creation, having only a resonating awareness and no ego, can't be apart from you, can't be separate, and having no ego, is incapable of attachments, and conditions. Creation has no conflict with anything you say you want. Creation says *"yes"* to *all* your choices. Imagine that. Creation works ultimately for the truth of your Soul. Therefore, Creation will bring to you experiences that are certain to challenge your most cherished illusions about yourself and challenge your most inflated denials of truth. Since very few of us know the truth of our Soul, we have to begin with where we are at and this is why it is important to begin with no self-condemnation. We learn by going where we believe we want to go and we end by meeting our Soul's truth in a place we really want to reside. And often this means we end up where we started from but with a new awareness, new eyes and a new heart, and a new appreciation of the life we have.

Imagine that Creation has one goal—for all of Creation to know Love. Human beings are a contradiction—a polarized consciousness—conceived in Grace, Blessed by the Intelligence and Beauty of Creation—and afraid of life and death. Human beings are a strange and wondrous piece of work. It is vital that we notice the transformative beauty—the beauty that human beings at all levels of life are capable of manifesting. It is vital that human beings re-consider their relationship with Creation.

What does Creation, which is Consciousness itself, see when it looks at you? Creation sees your beauty, your intelligence, and your truth. Creation also sees your ulterior motives, your hidden agendas and gives them to you in order that you may see them. Creation sees the new existence you desire and says, "Yes." Creation sees the old existence you hold on to and says, "Yes."

It is literal truth that everything you do is a choice. And that Creation says yes to all your choices, no matter what they are. You can choose to believe that you are at the mercy of outside forces and don't have a choice or you can choose to make conscious choice and consciously expect them to manifest.

Practice looking at your life as if everything is a deliberate choice. When you feel angry, say to yourself, "I choose to be angry." However dire the feeling is, say, "I choose to feel picked-on. I choose to obsess on damage. I choose to obsess. I choose to feel like I don't have a choice. I choose to be anxious about outcomes." Pretty weird. Stand before your mirror, look yourself in the eye and say, "I choose self-pity." This is a very hard practice. But it is a high form of self-inquiry and what is revealed in such a practice accelerates transformation in unimaginable ways.

Would anyone deliberately make these choices? Yes, some part of you does. If you were not making those choices, victim and conflict would not exist in your life.

Remember—if you don't want it, stop calling it. If you don't want it, don't feed it.

All manifest life comes ultimately from the Source of Love and Grace, Beauty, Intelligence, the Source of Consciousness itself. Your relationship with that Source is in your relationship with your Self. Your Thou. Practice gratitude and patience in all your relationships. Choose to receive Wisdom, Intelligence, Love and Grace. And look into your own eyes and say, "I choose to let go of any self-condemnation that resides in me." and then smile at yourself and say, "I choose Blessing."

CHAPTER ELEVEN

EVOCATIVE QUESTIONS FROM PRIVATE SESSIONS

Student Question: "It is often said in spiritual and new age writings that beliefs are the cause of suffering. Would you say it is true that beliefs cause suffering? And could you explain?"

Beliefs can cause suffering and suffering can create beliefs. If you are looking at cause, it would be more accurate to say that outcome thinking, conditions and expectations about the future, cause suffering. Disappointed expectations and holding on to attachments are the greatest cause of suffering in the world.

What do people generally tell themselves when they are suffering? They often try to figure out the cause of their suffering so that they know who or what to blame. They say, "Why me?" They try to manipulate blame hoping to make their suffering go away. We all have done this. We say, *"So-and-so or such-and-such is responsible for my suffering, therefore so-and-so and such-and-such must be punished, must change, must be destroyed, so that I will no longer suffer."* This is manipulative thinking. This is conditioned thinking. This is outcome thinking.

Outcome thinking means you are focusing and projecting your attention toward future outcomes and toward how to make those outcomes happen—or how to prevent those outcomes from happening. You invest a lot of emotional energy toward those outcomes that are sheer fantasy and might never happen. Attachment to outcomes is based on conditions and expectations and in the sense that conditions and expectations come from your beliefs about reality, beliefs do cause suffering. But the actual cause is outcome thinking—holding expectations and conditions about a future which might never come true.

The beliefs that we carry in our consciousness are conditions that we have arrived at over many years and these conditions have to do with our relationship with life itself. These conditions set-up expectations about outcomes and direct our attention toward outcomes that will fulfill our conditions. Because beliefs are often based on false evidence, beliefs create false assumptions and false conclusions, which lead to false outcomes—and false outcomes create further false evidence that loops back to and supports the beliefs.

Obsession with outcomes promotes *indirect living*, where rather than just simply living life as it happens in the moment, you are talking to yourself about life, about what you missed and what you lack and what you need and why you don't have it and how you have to be to make sure you get it and who has what you should have and how to get yours and make sure life can't hurt or scare you again . . . .

This endless commentary is exhausting and accounts for some of the tiredness that accompanies transformation—you are trying to manifest change but you have a consciousness in your head directing all your stories, like *"this goes here and this goes there and this is about lack and this is about victim and this is what should have happened and this is what needs to happen and this is what might happen and this had better happen and this better not happen and you should do this and they did that but they should do this so that this can happen . . . . and if this doesn't happen I will have to make sure this other thing happens and I had better have an escape plan in case this one doesn't happen right . . . And this is what it all means and I have to know what the other thing means before I can be safe because it all means something and until I know what it all means I won't be safe . . . ."* This makes life very complicated and exhausting.

When you let go of the immediate cause of suffering, which is attachment to outcomes, suffering decreases because instead of an anxious emphasis on future outcomes your view of reality becomes one of quiet, strong acceptance of the moment—with no desire to manipulate the moment in the hope that the manipulation will lead to the outcome you want. Patient willingness to receive truth and patient trust in the appropriate outcome happening in its appropriate time replaces judgment, anger, bitterness, blame, hostility, guilt—these feelings that arise from disappointed expectations. You now understand that if you are in something for the fantasy outcome, or so that you can control the outcome, or for what you hope to get from it—the hope that it will fulfill all your expectations—you miss the possible miracle.

Miracle is always available. Miracle comes from true evidence. True evidence is not extraordinary, is always available, and is always happening. One of the best definitions of miracle I have read comes from Willa Cather. "Miracles rest not so much upon faces or voices or healing power coming to us from afar off, but on our own perceptions being made finer, so that our eyes can see and our ears can hear what was there about us always."

Student Question: "We are trained to believe that beliefs are all-important. What's the point of all this controversy? How do we know what to believe?"

The "controversy" comes from the fact that beliefs are often a source of conflict and violence in the world, between nations, and in the lives of individuals. Spiritual teachers have been declaring for centuries—in some form or another—that beliefs, rather than creating unity, divide people; that toxic beliefs can lodge in our cells, in our muscles and bones for centuries creating disease, and that we must be willing to let go of the importance we give to beliefs.

Don't be attached to belief yet know that you can *choose to believe* anything that your own experience tells you is nurturing, strengthening, or inspiring.

Look at this as . . . say you break a leg, you put it in a cast for protection and to keep the limb in proper alignment so that it can heal. A belief can serve in the same way, to give support, a protective shield while you grow. *But, you don't put a cast on a broken leg and leave it there forever and say that the leg can't function without the cast.* At some point, you let go of the cast so the leg can breathe, grow, complete its healing, and develop its strength.

So it is with your consciousness. You wouldn't knowingly keep your consciousness in a cast. But this is what we do when we cling to beliefs that limit life, growth, healing; beliefs that prevent expanded awareness. We, as a species, are suffocating in our ego/derived casts. Fixating on a rigid, controlling belief is like trying to keep your intelligence and creativity—your self-inquiry, your self-awareness, your truth, your joy—in a cast and saying you can't function without the cast. Keeping your cast intact requires that you keep yourself *unavailable to new information and new experience.* To stay unavailable you have to turn away from revelation, turn away from truth about yourself and others that would permit expanded awareness. Where does that leave us as a species? All the strategies we evolve to keep the cast intact create a consciousness that is rigid, controlling, and that is referred to, in spiritual language, as self-importance.

What is self-importance?

Self-importance is the *action* of the ego, tightening, closing up and resisting self-inquiry. Self-importance is characterized by self-pity or self-righteousness. Self-importance is characterized by being offended by the words and actions of your fellow human beings; by how deeply you take things personally; and by the strength of your attachment to your own beliefs and judgments. Self-importance demands approval and validation from the world, and demands that you always be "right" in the eyes of the world. This requires you to spend a lot of time and energy "explaining" yourself to others, defending your judgments and proving that others are wrong or dangerous and that you are right.

Self-importance requires that you go through life offended by someone or something all the time. Self-importance requires that you find significant "others" who will validate your identity and who will be always willing participants in your psychodramas. This is often called *relationship* and *friendship* in the human ego-dictionary. Be always willing to let go of self-importance when you recognize it in yourself.

The beliefs that let go in the transformative process are those self-negating beliefs that live deep in your subconscious and unconscious and serve to keep your "cast" intact. Be willing to be free.

Student: "You mention self-importance a lot. I think I get it but just how do I recognize when I am being self-important? This is where I get mixed up."

How do you recognize self-importance? Embarrassment, resentment, petulance, feeling misunderstood and mistreated and blaming others for that, guilt and defensiveness, a feeling that you are not receiving what you are owed. These qualities are an indication that your ego-centered beliefs have been activated.

Self-importance has to do with your fear of being judged, your fear of being wrong, and your determination to prove that you are right. Think of all the weird stuff that you are capable of doing when you are embarrassed, resentful, and defensive. Don't condemn yourself, you are just trying to be safe. *Practice giving yourself the freedom to be wrong.* What if you were never afraid to be wrong? There is nothing you wouldn't be willing to try or be able to accomplish.

Self-importance has many polarities. You could say it is the opposite of any feeling and expression of true well-being. Self-importance is the opposite of gratitude. Self-importance means that you spend most of your life offended by others. Self-importance is characterized by self-righteous indignation, an attachment to being right, an inability let go of judgments, a constant inquisition into other people's motives—a constant interpretation of what motivates others. Self-importance is self-pity and a constant search for vindication and a constant compulsion to make others "wrong" so that you can be "right". Self-importance is an exaggeration of natural human qualities, like the natural human interest in other humans. It is a very subtle and exaggerated narcissism.

The opposite of self-importance is accountability and impeccability. Accountability means you accept your responsibility for everything—the good and the bad—that *you* create. Impeccability does not mean that you are always right, it means that you are always true. How do you recognize when you are being true. A feeling of peace and certainty. A sense of walking in beauty as a constant inner way of life. A sense of happiness. Self-importance is the opposite of happiness.

SAME STUDENT: "But isn't arrogance the real sign of self-importance? Isn't that how you tell when someone else—or even yourself—is lost in self-importance?"

Self-importance is characterized by unconscious fear. And this kind of fear is often accompanied by arrogance which is used to disguise the fear—sometimes an obvious bravado, whistling in the dark and sometimes a very subtle arrogance, but yes, you could say arrogance is the nature of the ego.

Both fear and arrogance are part of your egoic hidden agendas—the energy of hidden belief clusters. These hidden agendas keep you *separate—separate from God, separate from other human beings*—and keep you in a state of withholding, guarding, distrusting, controlling, yourself and others—fearful of giving any part of yourself away. You may observe your self-importance by noticing when you feel offended, when you are defensive or distrustful, when you feel that there are special differences in you that make you separate, or better than, or worse than, or set apart from in some special way, the average person—either in a superior way or an inferior way as self-importance can express as either an inferiority complex or a superiority complex—both are one and the same and either way you are defining yourself at a deep level as separate and different from others.

One of the polarities of self-importance is empathy, connectedness and love. You may create a sense of connectedness in yourself by practicing unity. You practice unity by making it a point B on your consciousness map—practice self-acceptance, stop judging yourself and comparing yourself to others, keep letting go of a competitiveness that compels you to judge others and constantly try to outdo others and feel that you are better than them—either in your own mind or outwardly in the world.

Self-importance is an expression of your belief in lack, your belief that fear is terminal and will never go away, your belief that your fear needs constant management, your belief that you need to constantly protect yourself from potentially damaging others. Practice letting go of your belief that you lack something, that you lack *anything*. Let go of any belief that your marginal existence—your separateness, your fearful belief in dangerous others, your belief that you cannot change your existence, your belief that something from outside of yourself is responsible for your choices, for your existence, and for your safety. And let go of the belief that the hollow feeling of fear and lack within you means that the world owes you, that the world has to fill you by

...... INSTITUTE LIBRARY
57 Post Street
..... Francisco, CA 94104
.415) 393-0101

fulfilling your expectations and conditions. The true opposite—*polarity*—of self-importance is freedom.

Student: "I have been working with the thought for the day—and the first waking thought—and both thoughts are about peace—but it seems like I am having more bad dreams—or maybe it is that I am more aware of my bad dreams. Is there a focus that can help me work with this?"

Sometimes the bad dreams must release before the true dreams can manifest. It is often part of the process of transmutation that when you create a mantra—a Word of Power such as peace—what will come up from the emotional depths is the place in you where there is neither peace, nor any belief that peace is possible. It is as if the lies must be seen before the truth can be revealed. You want to look at your nightmares as a process of releasing which is moving you toward peace and not as something wrong or something that has to be changed or fixed or even understood. Working with the waking thought and thought for the day practices is a powerful choice which creates a lot of energy. Work with bad dreams as if they are a power point and choose truth and beauty as the counterpoint to bad dreams. Choose to know that you can tap into the energy of peace in the midst of a bad dream. Don't think you have to process the bad dream, this is like processing *'feelings'* instead of processing focus on the practices. Practice conscious dreaming by knowing in the dream that you can choose blessing and peace and shift the bad dream into peace. Make that a mantra before going to sleep, choose to be able to take conscious action in your dreams and shift your bad dreams into peace.

We have been trained to believe that peace, health, joy, or serenity—the qualities of blessing—can only come with the removal of pain and conflict. So we believe we have to get rid of the pain or conflict first, *before* peace can come—therefore we focus on getting rid of conflict thinking, in our belief, that this the way to peace. And when bad dreams and bad feelings emerge after we have made a powerful choice (such as peace) we tend to think that something has gone wrong or that we are doing something wrong and so we focus attention on getting rid of what is wrong, when what we are experiencing is part of a natural and organic process toward truth.

And we have been trained to associate receiving with feelings of satisfaction or gratification. Peace has nothing to do with gratification or any such ego based quality. And peace is not a rare quality that can only exist in the absence of conflict. Peace is all around us and can be tapped into any time.

Peace is available every moment. There are no conditions on peace. Nothing has to change before you can receive peace, joy, feelings of abundance or love. You can experience peace right now. No matter what the outward experience; no matter what the outward event, you can feel peace or joy, love or bliss at any moment.

You can be in peace.
You can be in serenity.
You can be in Love.
Right now.
"In Love" does not mean with someone,
Love does not mean love *stories*,
Love, not love stories,
Love—
No matter what—
Love is always available.
Imagine that all your love stories are written by Wisdom.
Imagine that all your life stories are shaped by Beauty.
Imagine that all of your responses are moved by an Intelligence
    that streams from the Source of Intelligence Itself.
This is always available.
Imagine this—
All the time.

CHAPTER TWELVE
THE QUESTION AND ANSWER PROJECT

As a special project I often pass out questions which students can answer or not answer. These questions are designed to allow the students to test their own understanding of the fundamentals of Real Magic. Students develop their own language, their own understanding—nothing is expressed by rote, every answer is "correct" and each answer is individual.

It has been an interesting experience for me to see the creative energies involved in each student's individual understanding of each question. There are correct answers to some of these questions but the reader needs to realize that each student's experience is creative and comes from their own heart and soul. Therefore observe your own tendency to judge the "correctness" of the student answers and practice letting go of any judgmental tendencies.

I could write a book based on these Question/Answer projects but for this book I have selected just a few questions and three or four responses from students that serve as a complement to my teacher's commentary. My commentary is placed at the end of the student responses.

QUESTION: What is the difference between the words as you hear them in a lecture/lesson within a class context and the same words as you hear them in a taped, guided meditation?

STUDENT ANSWERS:

"When I look back on the Course and think about the lecture format versus the meditations, there's a whole different dynamic between the two structures. In a lecture/lesson format, it feels as if the ego (both collective and individual) is projected on the teacher/lecturer. Even if a facilitator is completely present, aware, and 'tuned in', he/she still has to be vigilant about ego projection. This need for vigilance can dilute some of the energy of the message as well as potentially distract the audience as a whole. Sometimes it feels like an energetic tug-of-war.

On the other hand that same information coming through meditation can be received by the group with much less resistance. If everyone has the intention of being in a receptive, open place, there will be a more unified effort on the group's part to contribute to the power of the message instead of struggling with it in the intellectual body. The essence of the information is still the same but it's delivered via a different path and diminishes the penchant for resistant by the ego.

Reading back on my above answer with lots and lots of theory, story, and way too many words, here's my distilled answer: it doesn't matter in what format the information is delivered. It's simply about the intention of both the giver and receiver. If the desire is to give pure truth, that's what happens either through meditation or lecture. If the intention of the listener is to hear truth, that is what will happen regardless of the form of delivery. Truth is truth—plain and simple. End of story."

"Frequency? This is what came to me when I stopped thinking about it. When *we* are listening in class, vs. receiving in a meditation, *our* frequency of vibration does change from one state to another, so when we are meditating we can *receive* the same words in a deeper, more energetic way. We can *focus* our awareness in meditation so that our interpretive mind stops analyzing the words, and become more truly conscious of the energy of those very same words. We can more *embody* the words in meditation, listening or speaking, if that makes sense."

"When something comes through in a meditation, I tend to UNDERSTAND it in a much more profound way. It's almost as if I understand it in a cellular level instantly. In a lecture or lesson, I think about it and then maybe I see instances where it makes sense, then slowly it gets absorbed into an understanding."

"The difference is only in my reaction—my *receiving*. I remember wonderful times when I have been very actively engaged in [your] lectures, when all my senses have been attuned to [your] words. If I listen attentively without critical processing, then these words become part of my maturing wisdom. In meditation, words bypass the belief and defense hang-ups I might have and assimilate cellularly/ emotionally and instantly. The words are the same—it's my reaction to the different modalities that is different."

"Lecture/lesson is focused on a collective consciousness and utilizes words, examples, experiences to teach more than one student at a time. I have also notice that at times a lesson or lecture can be about a topic or a particular student but in fact the teaching is for all. Each student comes to the information with a different set of learning to be received and the group guidance picks the appropriate vehicle to assist each student in getting to that. This is why classes can feel so impacting when it does not appear that all that much occurred. Spiritual Guidance coming through the teacher is working on a multi-dimensional level that we students are not always aware of.

My own experience is that through meditation I have learned greater awareness and thus wisdom, compassion, and love and that this has assisted me in being more available to the lecture information in classes. I think, though that the classes help me move forward in my practices and in letting go of separation which has assisted me in my meditations and direct communication w/ the Source."

"My intuition wants to say there is no difference in terms of quality or truth, however my experience is different and that is because of focus. In the lecture my focus is on the teacher and others outside of myself. In meditation my focus is turned inward and the words have an immediate impact. In the lecture/lesson my interpretive mind gets stimulated, I am listening and I have something going on in my head and I am also listening to other people's input. Another difference is that the lecture is instructive and, although it is happening, I am not aware of being brought to a higher vibration—my ego reacts to it (higher vibration) but I don't feel it. During the meditation I am aware of moving into higher vibrations."

COMMENTARY FROM THE TEACHER:

While resistance can occur, it is not really a problem for the teacher if the student is projecting resistance. That problem belongs to the student. So there is not a great need for vigilance on my part in terms of their resistance. Perhaps 10 per cent of my energy will be focused on observing *multidimensionaly* what is happening in the environment of the classroom. The greater part of my consciousness will be focused on transmitting the message whether or not it is a lecture or a meditation. So you see my experience is very different from the student's experience and there is no comparison.

The key word in meditation would be *intimate*. The ego-mind releases its hold on the heart and the person experiences a sense of intimacy with the Source—with an intimate Thou rather than an It. This does indeed have to do with focus. You could say that lecture has a mental focus; meditation has a multidimensional focus. And each experience has ultimately a multidimensional focus that merges in wholeness with itself and becomes a heart focus. It is true that in a lecture the student's interpretive mind is listening and judging while in a meditation the student's interpretive mind relaxes and there is less resistance to the experience.

But whoever said "frequencies" was correct. The class lectures are loaded with key words, words carrying *conscious frequencies* that prepare the students to receive the higher frequencies in the meditations. These are the frequencies which lead to revelation and self-knowledge. This is why, rather than answering questions, I constantly direct students to *"do your practices"*. Everything in the Course, everything in a class, every meditation, every practice, is a conscious creation that works to bring you into multidimensional wholeness—*if you pay attention to your experiences throughout the Course.* This is why you are constantly directed to let go of the interpretive mind—let go of looking for *meaning*!

Albert Einstein said that the intuitive mind is a sacred gift and the rational *[interpretive]* mind is a faithful servant. He went on to say that we have created a society that honors the servant and has forgotten the gift.

Meditation often feels more intimate and therefore more personally real because of this feeling of intimacy with the Source. Without the distractions created by trying to interpret the experience, your ego can experience the deep silence which is true experience.

In a lecture the interpretive mind is active—looking for meaning and thinking about content and context and locked in, for the most part, to a belief that meaning, content, and context are important and real. This focus on meaning is important in a limited way for making connections in the world of physical phenomenon but a focus on interpretation interferes with the receiving of Wisdom.

In a meditation the interpretive mind is (hopefully—this is the ideal) silent, not active so there is no part of mind looking for meaning and trying to interpret and second guess, trying to react to whatever threat or resistance the combined lecture/meditation might be bringing up in the student—all of which distracts from receiving Wisdom or Revelations.

The true context of your life is in revealed knowledge—revelation. When mental, emotional, and spiritual attention merge into one multidimensional awareness, revelation happens—truth is revealed through an organic creative process and the result is Wisdom. I break down the ways of processing information into two distinct processes—a psychological/intellectual/interpretive process and a creative/intuitive/spiritual process. These different ways of processing must merge in order to receive Wisdom because wholeness is necessary in the creation of a true functioning human being. There are times when it is necessary to think about the teachings and there are times when it is necessary to practice the deep and receptive silence that lives within the teachings.

Ideally, in the creative process of the Real Magic Course, the lectures and meditations and practices are equally important in preparing students for the merging of the two ways of processing information, for the merge into superconsciousness. This happens when class studies, meditations, and daily attention practices, are practiced in a constant, diligent, daily, way. With this integrated receiving comes a great assimilation of both experiences—both the lecture/interpretation studies and revelation of Wisdom. This is an integration in the brain that leads to Mastery. This is the Alchemy of Liberation.

QUESTION: Why is it to your advantage to polarize the energy of problems?

STUDENT ANSWERS:

"It creates a vessel where transmutation/change can happen. You utilize attention/ focus to create heat on Point B The more focus placed on "B", the more "A" collapses into "B" and an entirely new, stronger Truth is the result."

"It's in polarizing the energy of 'problems' that we transcend the loop of 'fixing' what's 'wrong', and become aware of our most desired state, which is literally pointed to *by* the "problem." Problems are our guides to Truth. *Polarizing the energy maximizes the energy available, by creating a structure for it.*"

"When you polarize the energy of your problems you create the opportunity for a new energy structure to come into being. It creates a vessel for the energy, a strong and focused structure to hold the energy within that structure so that it can be transmuted by the heat of your attention. It gives you a place to focus your attention on what you really want and away from that which makes you unhappy."

COMMENTARY BY TEACHER:

In the practice of alchemy it is necessary to create a vehicle or vessel where-in energy can be contained and gathered—where it can accumulate. This vessel must be strong enough to contain all the forces of energy that are at play in the process of transmutation. This vessel must be strong enough to hold the energy that is leaving and direct the energy that is coming into form. If either part of the vessel is weak—for instance if you are not clear about your Point A starting point—or if you are wobbly about the Point B result you want to receive—energy will leak into the environment and dissipate. You want a structure that will contain the energy and allow it to 'grow'.

This is why when you are polarizing a problem it is vitally important to look honestly at yourself and your situation and to let go of all the stories you have been telling yourself about your situation. When you create a polarity by giving yourself truth—by telling yourself what it is you really and truly want to let go of, and then turn to the opposite pole and declare what it is you want to receive into your life as a new existence, you create a powerful polarity that forms a strong alchemical vessel. And this polarity forms the vessel, the structure that contains and directs the necessary creative energy involved in the process of Creation. And this energy, contained and directed by this powerful structure, moves in your behalf to create an outcome that is the equivalent of something you really want to have.

And the creation of a polarity gives you the capacity to work with power points. The energies involved in a power point are the energies of opposing intentions—the fixed intention that created your current and past existence (Point A) *and* the chosen and new creative intention that builds the energy of a new existence at Point B. The energies of thinking in the old way and thinking in a new way are both present in a power point and you are in between those energies with a choice to make.

The energy of your old existence is a place where your attention is fixed in a description of reality—(the 'real' world)—that has been created within you from ancestors, parents, siblings, friends, teachers—the culture of your past merged with the culture of the times you live in. This creates a foundation reality that influences all the conclusions you arrive at within yourself as you, over the years, process all these factors that have been given to you and which make up your current world moment. This is what makes up the energy of your Point A. So your old existence can contain energies of great beauty, bliss and happiness that do not need transmuting and also contain energies that hold you in a marginal existence inside a haunted house. These, then, are the energies that become, at any given moment, a Point A in a polarity map.

When you create a potential new existence at Point B, you create a new approach to life, a conscious approach to creating that goes beyond the beliefs about life that reside in your old existence. In this new approach to life you learn to consciously focus your attention on fresh, new, intentions that have the power to dissipate and transmute your old existence. This is the reason why esoteric teachings such as the Hermetic Tradition have been considered dangerous by every form of social authority all the way from the beginning of the Christian, Hebrew, and Islamic Churches right up to the present social and religious authorities. The Hermetic Teachings are about true autonomy.

Whether or not the new intention is possible—and given the beliefs that still govern our old world they are not possible—is of no importance. What matters is the desire for a new existence that lives within the energies of Point B. These are the important energies that are involved in a power point—the energies of new intention, of thinking in a new way, of giving yourself something new and alive to focus new and conscious attention on—this is the energy that matters. This is why the feelings that come from your old existence do not matter.

Polarizing these energies gives your mind something to do beyond the problem, it creates both a new direction for your mind to focus on (the map) and a form (vessel) that will hold and use all the energies of what is leaving and what is emerging—as you in your daily life work consciously with all these tremendous energies that come awake as you practice the Real Magic practices. The successful working of power point energies gives you a solid foundation from which to welcome a new existence for yourself and for the world. This is why we are Radical!

The Law of Reversal, the Principle of Polarity, and Power Points are radical practices that actually accelerate change. And this play of forces in a power point has a great advantage in that it breaks the ego loop in our consciousness and the shift allows the ego to release its hold. This is radical.

These are difficult practices to master because you are truly mastering the energy of the moment, mastering the art of focusing your attention in a moment when you are reacting intensely to the past. You are living in the past and it is creating tremendous stress. As you do your practices, you are actually shifting the energy of stress tension into the energy of creative tension.

And it feels wonderful as you advance, to realize that you are in a vital moment, of vital power, vital creative energies. And when you experience the shifting of the energies in your power points it is like no other feeling you will ever experience. To actually feel it happen is so liberating. You become a true believer of the first kind—on the side of the angels! It is a truly liberating practice to Master the Moment.

QUESTION: What is meant by "your feelings don't matter"?

STUDENT ANSWERS:

"You cannot change the direction of the wind by analyzing the movements of a weather vane. Feelings are a weather vane."

"(this is one of my favorite questions) Feelings are just a reminder that energy is doing things. Don't fixate on feelings since that just feeds the ego and self-importance. Allow the feelings to flow—don't stay stuck!! Also, feelings are a great reminder that an unconscious belief is being triggered."

"Feelings are like the weather—they change continuously and come and go depending on our thoughts, where we focus our attention, external situations, hormones, how others are treating us, etc. While they may sometimes be helpful, it is important not to give them too much emphasis or be distracted by them. Sometimes feelings are helpful signals, clues to pay attention to something that is going on in my life that I may need to change. Sometimes they are deep and old and need to be expressed and released to clear the energy and open the way for transformation. What is important is to keep our attention focused on our choices and intention. This is where transformation (and Freedom!) takes place, not in the realm of moment by moment feelings."

"Our feelings help us detect where it is we are obsessing. If we use our feelings for this, then they are useful. We learn to use our feelings as a tool to move us beyond self-importance and into a place where we can choose what it is we really want. When we get stuck in our feelings, thinking they are what define our life, then they really don't matter! Our feelings are only fleeting glimpses of our selves, knee-jerking us around whether they are chaotic and happy or depressed and angry. When we can step outside these feelings and live in a steady and filled Life, then we understand that our feelings aren't what matter—our True Life is lived beyond our feelings and in spite of our feelings."

"I have observed that this is one of the more challenging concepts for students. It is wonderful because exactly what occurs when we (students) hear this statement is what this statement is asking us to observe and transform. "Your Feelings Don't Matter" is about awareness of Power Points—those vital moments where old beliefs and subsequent old feelings have been activated AND where there is an opportunity to release those old beliefs/feelings. By training ourselves to notice our emotional reaction and use mantras to transmute the energy we are freeing ourselves from the past. Your Feelings Don't Matter is freedom—freedom from what once was and freedom to be present to what the Universe is providing to us right now. I am able to notice my feelings, see them as energy, have them move through me and be free of the belief that what we experience as feelings is the truth. Truth is not our experience of our feelings, truth is awareness and love in being and receiving. Truth exists within and beyond what the ego says is real. Thus, the statement "Your Feelings Don't Matter" is also an experiential teaching for students. This phrase often activates old beliefs about how important our feelings are and if our feelings are not important then we as individuals must not be important (some version of this). Every time I hear this phrase I receive a teaching and opportunity to let go of self-importance."

"Your feelings *don't* matter—they are just the signal that an unconscious belief has been energized. The feelings tell you that it is time to use your tools to create something new, to transmute this old belief that has so much power into a new structure that brings you into more freedom and happiness. If you believe that your feelings matter then you will talk to yourself and others about your feelings and give them attention and support so that you are actually strengthening the structure of the old belief. The feelings are not the truth of which you are, they are only a clue to signify that something is up for review and if you don't want that feeling in your life it is an opportunity to create something new."

TEACHER COMMENTARY:

This comment (your feelings don't matter) is a statement I make in class for its shock value and it has become a Real Magic cliché. In this rational, interpretive, psychologically and mentally focused world, emotions are considered as powerful and are feared as irrational. And because it is true that emotions can be chaotic and messy and frighten onlookers, we are taught to repress them—which, as has been pretty well defined in the psychologically focused twentieth century, leads to mayhem at the inner levels. We are taught that feelings are powerful and that we must pay therapeutic attention to and *process* our feelings in order to understand ourselves and be psychologically whole.

The esoteric teachings have an entirely different outlook and approach to feelings and the Hermetic Teachings teach you to process feelings in a whole new way. This approach is almost the opposite of the psychological process. In this esoteric view of and approach to feelings, we are taught that feelings follow attention—arise from wherever our attention is most fixed. And the place where attention becomes most fixated is in our belief clusters. And *attention* both creates energy and follows energy and the first principle we are taught is that energy is what creates—energy does things, energy makes things happen—energy creates feelings.

Feelings are not bad. Feelings are the energy of our belief systems expressing through us when our attention energizes a belief. This can be confusing because our identity (and our self-importance) is so attached to our beliefs that we believe that our feelings are part of our *identity*. We feel them as if they are true *but* they are *not* true. They are not our identity. They are expressions of what we believe to be true about ourselves and the world.

Feelings are not bad. There is nothing wrong with feelings. Bliss is a feeling. Happy is a feeling. Feelings simply indicate that our energy is moving, doing things, reacting, responding. Our energy is reacting and responding constantly to both our *inner* attention and to the attention we give to (and receive from) our *outer* environment. Feelings arise when our deepest beliefs are stirred up, activated either by the inner movement of our thoughts and memories or activated by changes in our environment. This is why it is important to not take your feelings *personally*. This creates a distance.

So when I say your feelings don't matter, what I actually mean is, it doesn't matter what the something is that activated the feeling and it doesn't matter what the feeling actually is—what matters in that moment—which is a *vital* moment; a power point, when you are feeling intense feelings—is that in this moment of intense feeling, *you have the choice to transmute the feeling and the belief clusters which gave rise to and are attached to the feeling.* The feeling is pointing to an incredible opportunity to directly transmute your ego.

Of course, you also have the choice to retain and process and strengthen the feeling and this will strengthen the deep belief clusters that created the feeling. This moment when you stay in resistance to the teachings and the practices is also a choice.

This practice is not about denying feelings, it is to help you experience and realize that you are more powerful than your feelings—so please stop giving so much power to your feelings. Feelings and emotions really do not matter except as *information!* They contain and give you clues about what haunts you and is making you feel unconscious, unhappy, and powerless! This is the only thing that is important about feelings—they are informing you that you are holding on to toxic energies from the past and reminding you that you have the power to transmute those toxic energies. They remind you that you have a choice to make. That is the only-only-only-only thing that is important about feeling! Keep repeating this to yourself!

The choices you make in your vital moments—moments of power—will transmute fear and rage into serenity, will transmute self-doubt and anxiety into clarity and self-knowledge. This is what is important—not the feeling but the opportunity to choose that which gives your soul vitality. The feelings that come from the vitality of the soul are feelings of bliss, of deep happiness, deep-down abiding satisfaction and faith and grace—these are feelings that tell you *(inform you—feelings are information)* that you have brought yourself to life and you are home free! And good stories come from these feelings. Stories you can pass on and give to the world that will build an energy of truth and an energy of believing in good stories, good feelings.

So, since feelings are not necessarily bad, then stories about feelings are not always bad. There are feelings that you want to trust and stories that you want to trust.

I had a student once who, in a discussion of feelings and whether there is any feeling that we can trust answered with this: "The feeling that can be trusted is the feeling that comes when you have hit a home run out of the ball park and you are headed for home and the way is free and clear." Everyone in that class got it. The feelings that arise from your Point A existence are very different from the feelings that arise at Point B when you hit that home run out of the ball park and the ego is transcended in pure ecstasy! And that ecstasy, when it comes as a buildup, a gathering of energy at Point B, will stay with you and build even stronger energy until it becomes strong enough to transmute your old world feelings of fear and lack. And these are the good stories. Make your life a good story, a work of art.

QUESTION: What is the difference between focus and obsession; between focused attention and fantasy?

STUDENT ANSWERS:

"The difference between focus and obsession/focused intention and fantasy are that in obsession there is a feeling of anxiety, helplessness, and circular thinking—one is caught in an ego loop. When one is focused there is not a sense of urgency. With fantasy there is a story, specific actors and outcomes.

Focused intention leaves room for creation to create. And I've found that often the creations are beyond my wildest imaginings."

"Focus is the conscious action of bringing your attention to where you want it to be.

Obsession is allowing your attention to be dragged compulsively to some distracting thought, sometimes "comforting", sometimes "frightening", but always DISTRACTING. Obsession is like a mechanism for NOT being aware of where you truly are (an escape). Focus puts you where you truly are."

"Fantasy is an emotion driven daydream created to fulfill desires. It's hard to tell the difference between fantasy and focused intention sometimes, especially when the desire for change concerns other people as in a relationship. That is an area where fantasy can really take hold.

Focusing attention to create a new life, an ideal one imagined with good intentions, is not fantasy, but using the power of the imagination, to create energy and change. Energy shifts, consciousness changes and slowly the habitual act of choosing one thing over another, becomes more in line with gaining true achievements and getting out of sadness and beliefs in lack."

"There is a big difference between focus and obsession. In the RM course, when focusing attention around something you want (your intention), there is actually an expansion of awareness that occurs and with this you are available to receive information or truth. With this kind of focus, there is a strong intention, and it is deliberate, but it is without an expectation. With obsession, you are creating a tremendous amount of energy around a focal point, but there is an element of control, as in, "I must have it or I will not be OK." This type of concentrated focus is dangerous and does not allow for creation to unfold.

"Fantasy is about living your life trying to compensate for what you think you lack. Focused intention is about living your life as the magical mystery ride it truly is."

"The difference between focus and obsession is that when are focused you don't have expectations about outcomes. Your energy is flexible. With obsession there is an expectation for outcomes and the energy is fixed. Focused attention is not fantasy because you recognize the Point A reality of your situation, but you focus on the Point B with conscious faith and trust. In fantasy there is denial of reality, of truth. It is an escape from Point A."

"Focus means to point your attention at a point and keep it there. It doesn't think about the place it is pointed at, it is not judging it. It does not expect an outcome. It is not emotional. Focus just points energy in a direction and continually returns the energy to that point when it tries to wander off. It directs energy and it is available to receive information as well. It is an open line of energy that is giving and receiving at the same time. Obsession is outcome oriented, it needs one specific result. It has a strong emotional attachment to that outcome. The energy of obsession is fixed and projecting from the ego. It does not receive information. It overrides the truth and projects the egos desires onto a person or thing. It is completely ego driven."

"Fantasy is a story you tell yourself about what you feel is lacking in your life. It comes from your ego. It comes from feeling powerless to create what you want and it creates more powerlessness. It drains your energy resources. Focused intention creates a powerful energy line to what you want and overrides the old beliefs and structures of the ego to create something new from who you truly are."

TEACHER COMMENTARY:

This is a bit of a trick question because focus and obsession are pretty much one and the same in the sense that has to do what you are doing with your attention. When you are in focus your attention is either focused on a clear and emotionally detached point of focus—or—your attention is focused on emotionally loaded obsessive fantasies. The action is the same, the difference is that one is a conscious action that feels good and gives you energy and one is an unconscious action that exhausts you. Obsession is a powerful focus with an emotional center—such as delusionary thoughts and desires. Obsession doesn't always necessarily mean a bad thing but it is a powerful single pointed thought that always has an emotional theme—and the word obsess often refers to a destructive aspect of human attention. *Obsession is a powerfully focused unconscious emotionally centered attention.*

Any deep seated belief can lead to a powerful focal point that is always 'calling' your attention and this pull on your attention is usually unconscious and can be the center of your delusions and fantasies.

Obsession is an unconscious fantasy that is used to compensate for your feelings of a lack that cannot be fulfilled, a belief that is focused on what you need from others that you are not getting. A student once told me that obsessive fantasy was "self-importance gone insane" and I would say that addiction to fantasy is just that—a *compensation* for something you don't have that is out of your reach, something you feel can never be fulfilled any other way. Obsessive fantasy, since it is always derives from feelings of lack, contains a powerful emotional 'charge'. This addiction to fantasy can claim your attention to the point where the only place you truly 'live' is in your fantasy world. Such addiction requires tremendous energy to break out of. Addiction to fantasy does not allow you to experience self-knowledge. This is why it is important to let go of it, and it can have such a strong hold on your emotional reality that it requires a tremendous catalyst to create a break-through within your consciousness and thus can be very painful.

On the other hand, focus as it is used in the Real Magic Course, refers to a *conscious* action. The key difference would be in the word *conscious*—conscious focus is a deliberate action of directing your attention toward a specific result—it has no specific emotional theme, if it contains desire it is a conscious desire that has no attachment to specific outcomes.

The difference between focus and obsession is the difference between a clear choice to live a conscious life and a murky choice to live an unconscious life. So when you practice letting go of fear and anxiety about outcomes, letting go of taking things personally, letting go of putting conditions on your choices, you are letting go of the attachments—unconscious fixations—that lead to obsession and addiction to fantasy.

CHAPTER THIRTEEN

THE QUESTION AND ANSWER PROJECT

The next few questions are similar but have very subtle differences and for this reason I have placed them all in one chapter.

QUESTION:

This question is presented in three parts:

(a) What is the difference between attachment and discernment?
(b) How can you tell when you are attached?
(c) When you practice being true, how can you tell when your ego is actually deeply invested in the experience?

STUDENT ANSWERS:

"I associate discernment with clear observation . . . perceiving without judgment, without expectation. When I am attached to any perception, outcome, thing or belief, there is a belief that whatever I see, want, have or believe is "right" or "true". This is my ego grounded in yesterday's stories. I can tell that I'm attached (to a particular perception/outcome/thing/belief) when I get stressed out. I'm discovering that it's a sure sign that I'm not being open to receiving from the Universe when my emotional or physical body gets tied up in knots. When I feel this [tied up in knots stress] it is a signal for me to choose to let go. And when I become aware of my attachment, (by becoming aware of my stress) I am able to get beyond judging or beating myself up for having attachments. That is when I know that I have practiced discernment! Discernment creates space for new information to come in and keep energy moving to a higher vibrational level. Attachment is closing the door on the possibility of this creative flow."

"The minute you "think and believe" anything, your interpretive mind is at work, and you have created a separation between your Self and your thoughts. It's so funny, how that feeling of *"I'm getting It!"* is the doorway *out* of it. Being true is and filled with discernment, and Knowing. If you live in Truth, your interpretive mind becomes a tool for organizing the revelations of Truth into intelligible forms. You can live in Truth and your ego can be expanded to contain Truth Consciousness. When interpretive mind has become discerning Mindfulness, there is no more separation."

"To me, attachment is to be emotionally invested in something, whether it be a person, situation, outcome, or way of being. Discernment is more like seeing all the parts of a situation, experience etc. with an open, nonjudgmental observing eye and noticing what is, seeing truth, because there is no ego involved. You can tell that you are attached when you feel things like fear, anger, frustration, stress, if the thing you want doesn't play out the way you think it should. You might think and believe that you are being true because these things that you are wanting are worthy and wonderful, but often when you receive a revelation it is that you have put conditions on the things you are trying to manifest."

"You know you are attached when you take things personally. You then act from fear and stress. You have expectations about outcomes and want to control what happens. You don't trust. This question provoked further questions for me. For instance is there a mental ego and an emotional ego? It seems to me that there is an emotional egoic way to react to situations as well as the mental interpretive mind egoic way to attach to situations. Are there more aspects to ego? It seems to be very unconscious and very subtle at times very difficult to comprehend how it is manipulating."

"I have been looking at discernment a lot these days. The difference between attachment and discernment is—when I'm attached I'm invested in the outcome and not fully present and so not available to receive truth. When I'm discerning, I'm open, present, observing, listening and able to receive truth on many levels and I find the response that comes is absolutely perfect and at times surprises the willies out of me! Awareness is leading me, I am receiving and truth shows up. It's unmistakable."

COMMENTARY FROM THE TEACHER:

Attachment has to do with a focus on outcomes and is usually accompanied by anxiety or fear. You can tell that you are attached when you have a lot of anxiety about outcomes and you spend a lot of time and energy processing this anxiety.

Discernment contains an awareness of possible outcomes but no emotional investment. When you are emotionally invested, you will be willing to expend enormous amounts of energy trying to make particular outcomes happen in particular ways. This is packed with conditions. Discernment does not think in a conditional way. Discernment is detached and observing and true discernment goes beyond observing into Knowing. The quality of discernment leads to wisdom.

In order to tell when your ego is deeply emotionally invested in outcomes that *have* to happen, observe where your fear is lodged, by observing what you are taking personally. The key to developing discernment is to practice letting go of attachment to outcomes and letting go of taking things personally.

In response to the above question from a student about aspects of the ego, what is ego? Just imagine that the ego is one consciousness and that all the parts of this consciousness—emotional and mental; unconscious and sub-conscious—function as one. They are one and the same because, although the interpretive mind is a monkey, and it runs all over the place trying to dodge or interpret and control the emotional content of any experience, the emotion itself is felt *instantaneously* with the experience. That which we call the mental ego and the emotional ego experience the experience as one highly impacting feeling.

In other words, if you hit your thumb with a hammer instant awareness runs through you—but after the sensation of awareness comes the reaction and that reaction can be that you breathe and count to ten or you scream and yell and curse and break something. Both reactions come from your ego which is both *feeling* the impact (emotion) and *interpreting* the impact (mental). You will either feel threatened or you will feel a more simple reality of observation. But the experience itself is an instantaneous physical/emotional impact—pain and awareness that your thumb has been hit with a hammer—*then* you react. Some people rage and try to kill the hammer in a desire to blame something! Some people stop and breathe, count to ten and consciously relax. Each of these reactions—paranoia or serenity—come from your interpretation of reality. Each interpretation comes from the program carried deep within your consciousness—and we call this program 'ego'. And the program that lives in your egoic consciousness is—protect and preserve the existing program.

You see, after the initial shock of physical pain comes emotional shock and the interpretive part of your consciousness goes to work to tell you what to do with the energy of emotion/pain/shock. This is the point where you react. The reaction happens in a split second and you are in it before you know it.

This is why a power point is so powerful. In this instant—vital moment—you are working with some old conclusions about life that live in your deepest realms of consciousness but which are telling you how to react to a particular situation—in other words, how do you react when you hit your thumb with a hammer? If you keep your head, you can shift the old energy that is working in you at that moment. You can shift from knee-jerk rage into serene discernment. You can lose your head or keep your head.

The ego is one consciousness with one function—to keep you safe and whole, to maintain one single identity. It functions in two parts, emotional and mental and it functions multidimensionally—it touches all dimensions of your consciousness from your toe nails, skin, heart, lungs, liver, to your astral (emotional) and mental dimensions—all parts of you are touched by the ego's movement in each instant. All your parts are part of a single consciousness that has its own multidimensional way of functioning—it is actually a single functioning consciousness. All of it is always present.

In terms of attachment and discernment we are looking at two different approaches to reality. It is possible to be attached to what constitutes reality for you and in this case, your ego would be working hard to keep all of you, even your attachments, safe and unmolested, untouched. Discernment comes from a well-tuned sense of reality and a well-tuned ability to *observe* reality without becoming *attached* to any particular aspect of it. Since reality is determined by the ways we have chosen to *define* our experience, then reality is arbitrary and depends entirely on subconscious beliefs *about* our experience. In which case, discernment would depend on your ability to transcend reality, to transcend prevailing beliefs and just simply *see what is transpiring without interpreting it emotionally.*

It has been argued that discernment is not truly possible in this polarized world of emotional scape-goating, of looking for blame, of deeply wounded love and neediness. If, on the other hand, reality is determined by beliefs and can be changed by transmuting the energy of our beliefs, then reality can be determined by our thoughts toward consciousness, therefore any thought that chooses discernment makes discernment possible. This allows discernment, as a quality, to live and grow within your consciousness. You can create a discerning mind within your own brain by working with these principles and consciously choosing to receive the quality of discernment.

In other words, you can create a real discernment in yourself by letting go of attachment to outcomes and attachment to any particular world view or any particular belief about reality you might be carrying. You create discernment by constantly polarizing self-importance (by letting go of taking things personally) and choosing discernment in the moment. Just keep doing your practices and one day, discernment will manifest and surprise you. And it will be part of your identity forever because your ego is protecting it!

QUESTION: Why do I ask you to *not* look for meaning?

STUDENT ANSWERS:

"Looking for meaning is an intellectual phenomenon, not an intuitive one. It puts you in the middle of process and is excessively focused on 'how' instead of 'what' you want to create."

"Looking for meaning engages the interpretive mind, which has a tendency to obscure if not obliterate awareness of Reality. "What does this mean" is one of those New Age questions that seem to lead the seeker right down the wrong path into their old stories and fantasies again."

"Looking for meaning engages the interpretive mind and "the greatest interference between the human being and Freedom is the interpretive mind." (A wonderful Sylvia quote.)"

"Looking for meaning deadens the truth behind the event, dream, poem, vision, art or experience. In the search for meaning the special quality of being is sucked into mental mazes and games."

"Looking for meaning will get you caught up in process. Focus on process creates more process. Focus on process blocks the energy of creation. When you look for meaning you get stuck in process and you stop creating."

COMMENTARY FROM TEACHER:

In our psychological and mental world, the focus of our training is on the interpretive mind. This is a focus on *how to interpret* the world rather than how to create and experience a world of truth and beauty. "Looking for meaning" is focused on *processing* the world rather than experiencing the world. A focus on creating the world comes from a place of knowing who you are and there is authenticity in it. And the authenticity itself brings true meaning to you as wisdom and self-knowledge. Only if you have self-knowledge will your experiences be true.

From the time we are born our parents, relatives, teachers, peers, are all busy teaching us how to interpret the world—describing for us how and what to be, how to act, how and what to think, how and what to believe and feel—how to define who we are within the existing world, training the ego how to keep the world from changing. Our interpretive mind is so corrupted by all the stories we've incorporated about how things are and who we should be, and so confused by this constant search for the *right* way to do things, the *right* meaning, that very few people actually experience what they actually think and feel and what life actually means to them—they are too busy interpreting the world according to the established template.

I suggest that you let go of looking for meaning because *not* looking for meaning is on a par with not looking for process—it is tied in with letting go of process. If you are trying to interpret the process of each thing in your crowded head, it is like stopping a tennis match (or any athletic event) in the middle of a play in order to analyze the game instead of just watching the game—you are never going to have anything but process—and the game will never be finished—which of course drives the brain into a dead end of chaos and aborted attempts to control chaos.

The new thought process within the Real Magic Course and the Hermetic Teachings gives your brain a chance to breathe, stretch, experience its power to create worlds in a healthy and rewarding way (as opposed to an addiction to fantasy way), and ultimately experience freedom. Once the brain itself has experienced freedom, nothing can stop us from the Walk in Beauty that is our birth right.

QUESTION: What is the difference between observing and interpreting?

STUDENT ANSWERS:

"Observing is noticing *what is* with no commentary, story or judgement about it. Interpreting is making up a story, looking for meaning, or placing a judgment on what is.

Example: It's a cloudy day and it's starting to rain. Vs. It's depressing, miserable weather today and I'm going to get soaked when I go to the store then I'll probably catch a cold . . ."

"In observing, there is simply a noticing of what is, without judgment attached to it. With interpreting, there is a lot of mind chatter. Your analytical mind is forming judgments and opinions based on your own particular belief systems and feelings."

"Observing is seeing what is really there without judgment. Observing just notices what is. It lets you see without the ego filter that distorts the truth. Interpreting is looking at something and making a choice about whether it is good or bad, right or wrong. It comes from your ego and creates a distortion of what is true in that moment."

TEACHER COMMENTARY:

Interpretation almost always has some degree of emotion attached to it. It is often an attempt to create the right story, a story that either supports the correct political, social, or spiritual, stance you want to take in regard to an experience—or a story that refutes the experience. It is *almost* always biased by your life experience, on your interpretation of the world. This means you subconsciously reach into your deep beliefs to judge each experience, each piece of information, to either reject it as not resonating with your identity, or accept it as "true". Your interpretive skill helps you determine what belief is most true and where to stand with it.

This conjures a lot of emotion which reinforces the stance you have taken. The purpose of emotion is to "fix" a story—emotion is the glue that fixes your stories in place in your consciousness where it becomes a part of your identity and you can remember who you are—or who you *think* you are. Once a story is created it merges with the existing belief structure and reinforces the belief. This is why I direct you to let go of your interpretive mind. Don't take any stance but open-ness and a willingness to change in authentic and creative ways.

A good practice with this is to stand in front of a mirror and ask the person in the mirror, "Who do you think you are?" And you will find yourself telling yourself stories.

Honing your objective observer skills gives you a way to view the world that is not colored by your belief system—by who you think you are. Observation is an eye that records what is going on around you without interpreting it emotionally. At some level we must use our interpretive mind but we use it as a skill that helps us to notice what is and not as the guide that interprets the personal meaning of what we notice. In a discerning mind, interpretation can have the same clarity of purpose that your intelligent intention to know who you are has.

For example, in class I ask you to practice noticing new places or walk down the street and notice the street as if you have never seen it before. Walk into a room and notice: "*This room is dominated by a red couch, the walls are beige, there is small blue-grey sofa in front of the east window, and the drapes are beige with blue-grey stripes that match the small sofa and walls . . . .*" Just give yourself the facts. especially when you are in a new situation or place. Practice this with no attempt to interpret what you see in a personal way.

If you were interpreting the room your emotional reactions coming from old stories would be saying: "*I don't like that much red, this person isn't a very good* *designer . . . there is nothing balancing all that red and the room is too small for this huge red thing . . . and I hate that color anyhow. What was she thinking when she bought that couch! This room is really uncomfortable . . . it is just like her and wow! I know more about color than she does . . . "*Interpreting from an old emotional stance requires that we take things personally and constantly compare ourselves to others! If we persist in taking everything personally, the quality of discernment does not have a chance to come home to us.

QUESTION: What is the difference between judgment and discernment?

STUDENT ANSWERS:

"Knowing (with a capital "K") doesn't have any aspect of analysis to it; it's not an intellectual process. Knowing is a quiet place full of pure discernment.

Judgment is rigid and filled with interpretation. It's usually rooted in the past and ego-driven."

"Discernment is observing in the sense of allowing revelation to occur without interpreting it. Judgment is an action that follows interpretation, and comes down on one side or another of that interpretation—a thing is either good or bad according to a set of beliefs."

"Discernment is being aware of what is and making choices about what kind of relationship we want to have with what is—which often has to do with the behavior of another person. Judgment is making up a story about what is happening and believing the story as good or bad, right or wrong, etc. Discernment has an energy of clarity and a light touch, wisdom and compassion. The energy of judgment has a heaviness, a self righteous and condemning quality to it."

"The difference between judgment and discernment is that with judgment, your own beliefs, attitudes, likes and dislikes come into play. With discernment, you are existing at a higher level of consciousness. This information is not clouded by the ego's preferences and attachment to outcomes."

"Discernment is looking at what is in front of you and seeing the truth in it without the ego's need for the truth to look any certain way. Discernment doesn't have an agenda about what the truth should be. Judgment comes from the ego and it needs to find a label and a box to fit everything into to make it feel strong. It projects from the ego and distorts what is true like interpretation does. It keeps the ego strong and separate. It feeds the belief in separation."

TEACHER COMMENTARY:

This is another trick question. And it looks as if none of these answers is correct except in a subjective sense—very personal. In Webster's Dictionary, discernment is defined as keen, perceptive and insightful *judgment*. Judgment is not the opposite of discernment, judgment is an *action* that can be discerning or it can be influenced by reactionary and egocentric interpretations of reality. Either way, judgment is a summing up, a conclusion about reality that is arrived at through many channels. Judgment is not necessarily an egoic reaction but the word *judgmental* it is often associated with reactionary thinking and in this case has come to mean a reactionary—which means fearful, jumping into blame, scape-goating, vengeful, projecting—approach that is unconcerned with accuracy or truth. This is a reactionary way of looking at the world and especially a reactionary way of looking at other people. When we say someone is too judgmental we often mean that person is coming from an unfair, fearful, place where their self-important consciousness is sitting in judgment.

Most usually judgment is a term used to define political or judicial conclusions. A *judge* is one who has been given the authority to, once a jury has come to a conclusion, pass judgment on the accused—but the accused is considered innocent until proven guilty. This is the judicial use of judgment.

In the Real Magic Course we work to create the quality of discernment in ourselves so that our judgments of a situation are not coming from a fearful, angry, projecting blame, reactionary, *interpretation* of events. Discernment gives us intelligent insight into events. Discernment requires that we practice clear sight, practice looking at reality in a non-personal, detached, way that is based on trust. Discernment is something that grows within you as you walk a path of being true to yourself and practice intelligent understanding of your own process. Discernment is something we come to trust as we become more and more true to ourselves. Its highest quality is intelligence. Discernment comes as we practice Wisdom. Discernment is a judgment that is coming from Wisdom. *"A keen, perceptive, and insightful judgment."*

So we could say that when judgment is coming from egocentric interpretations, beliefs and fears, it is reactionary but when judgment is coming from discerning wisdom it is true—authentic, accurate, and just.

Judgment is one of those words like process, interpret, and think. We all judge, interpret, process, think about and perceive the world around us. And we are trained to do this in a limited way, a way that limits our imagination and spiritual creativity. What I have done in creating the Real Magic Course is given us an approach to life that allows us to transmute our old, reactionary ideas, reactions, and beliefs and bring the qualities of discernment and wisdom to creative life within us.

We will still judge, interpret, process, and perceive, this is inherent in our intelligence, but we do it from a place of an intelligent understanding of what those processes really mean. We don't stay attached to our old and separatist ways of interpreting and processing information. We learn to think in a new way. We choose to move in Beauty, Truth, Empathy, Compassion, and Wisdom and allow those choices to come alive in us as we transmute our old reactionary ways and allow our true nature to come to life—our true House of Light. This is possible. Believe it.

CHAPTER FOURTEEN

RADICAL LIGHT

What does 'as above; so below' really mean? The relationship between macrocosm (above) and microcosm (below) is the key to the Hermetic Teachings. Macrocosm refers to the Eternal Reality of Light; the realm of God. Microcosm is its reflection; a fragmentation of Light; the world of human existence and human ego. The core of the Mystery School teachings throughout the centuries has been focused on reassembling the fragmented body of Light in human consciousness and uniting 'below' with 'above'. This is the Great Work.

We are at a crossroads time in history and it is important to keep in mind that the work we do—the Great Work of transmuting our egos and reassembling our Body of Light—is planetary work and each moment of truth that unfolds to fill our hearts shines forth from us as a beacon to light the way for those who come after.

It is important, as we work, to acknowledge the teachers and students down through the centuries who have walked The Hermetic Way in whatever form it appeared to them in their particular moment in history. They walked the Western Way and their pathwork created footsteps of Light for us to follow. The beauty of Hermes is that he appears to each generation in the form most needed at the time. He appears, bringing his knowledge of Light; his deep and abiding love for the Light of God and his faith that no matter how lost we might become as a species, there will always be a body of Light Bearers whose love for the Reality of Light and Wisdom is so great that they are willing to do whatever it takes to bring the Light home and bring the children home to the Light.

What does that mean for us as Walkers of the Hermetic Way? The Real Magic Course is a Path of Light. What is Light? Light is consciousness. Light is the language of consciousness. Light is the means by which subtle increments of information can circulate from *Above* to *Below* and Below to Above. All the information; all the patterns of existence; all the levels, and the information each level needs in order to live a balanced existence, is stored as filaments, beads, strings of Light—beyond words, beyond ideas, Light is the truest means of communication between us and Creation and us and other Life Forms.

It is easy to imagine that the Hermetic Teachings are the First Manifest Teachings. And it is just as easy to imagine that DNA is the first manifest Light—the first manifest form—the first genetic coding. And this is why we love Light. The affinity that we as human beings share with Light calls us all to share with each other our experiences of Light so that the channels of Light between us may be strengthened and that Living Light pour into every heart.

This is our birthright. Light is *manifest* Consciousness—the means by which Higher Consciousness communicates with human consciousness—our spiritual coding that incorporates more and more intelligent information as we follow our Soul through each Journey of Light.

The Egyptian Masters declared that our Soul is a Living Star, and this Light, the Star of our Soul, shines always as a beacon that lights our human path to a living Source of Light. It uplifts and inspires our hearts to move us onward toward the Source of Who We Are—the always present, unchanging Radical Light within.

I can imagine the Presence of Hermes, of Jesus, of Sophia, walking with us—walking in Light. Aware of us as we are aware of them. I take heart and I hope you will too, from these last words of Hermes, written thousands of years ago in praise to his God, *Atum,* and offered to us in this beautiful translation by Timothy Freke and Peter Gandy: Their book *The Hermetica*, is my bible and I have gone through more than one treasured, lop-eared, and much cherished copy.

"I am your instrument, and your wisdom plucks music from me,
I sing a song of my soul for your love has reached me.
You have made me a new being
. . . a fountain bubbling with Life.

Language is inadequate.
The gods sing a hymn of silence;
And I am silently singing"

END

135.45   Bennett, Sylvia
B472   Radical light

LaVergne, TN USA
20 October 2010
201614LV00004B/109/P

Mechanics' Institute Library

3 1750 03381 2317

9 781450 049337